DRAMA CLASSICS

The Drama Classics series aims to offer the world's greatest plays in affordable paperback editions for students, actors and theatregoers. The hallmarks of the series are accessible introductions, uncluttered and uncut texts and an overall theatrical perspective.

Given that readers may be encountering a particular play for the first time, the introduction seeks to fill in the theatrical/historical background and to outline the chief themes rather than concentrate on interpretational and textual analysis. Similarly the play-texts themselves are free of footnotes and other interpolations: instead there is an end-glossary of 'difficult' words and phrases.

The texts of the English-language plays in the series have been prepared taking full account of all existing scholarship. The foreign language plays have been newly translated into a modern English that is both actable and accurate: many of the translators regularly have their work staged professionally.

Under the editorship of Kenneth McLeish, the Drama Classics series is building into a first-class library of dramatic literature representing the best of world theatre.

Series editor: Kenneth McLeish

Associate editors:
Professor Trevor R. Griffiths, *School of Literary and Media Studies, University of North London*
Simon Trussler, *Reader in Drama, Goldsmiths' College, University of London*

DRAMA CLASSICS *the first hundred*

The publishers welcome suggestions for further titles

A DOLL'S HOUSE

by

Henrik Ibsen

translated and introduced by
Kenneth McLeish

NICK HERN BOOKS
London

A Drama Classic

A Doll's House first published in Great Britain in this translation
as a paperback original in 1994 by Nick Hern Books Limited,
14 Larden Road, London W3 7ST

Copyright in the translation from the Norwegian © 1994
by Kenneth McLeish

Copyright in the introduction © 1994 Nick Hern Books Ltd

Kenneth McLeish has asserted his moral right to be identified as
the translator of this work

Typeset by Country Setting, Woodchurch, Kent TN26 3TB
Printed in Great Britain by BPC Wheatons Ltd, Exeter

A CIP catalogue record for this book is available from the British Library

ISBN 1 85459 236 X

This translation was first performed by the English Touring Theatre in
spring 1994 directed by Stephen Unwin. Kelly Hunter played NORA,
Pip Donaghy HELMER, Robert Langdon Lloyd RANK, Ruth Mitchell
MRS LINDE, Sean Baker KROGSTAD and Helena McCarthy
ANNE-MARIE.

Introduction

Henrik Johan Ibsen (1828-1904)

When Ibsen was 23, he was appointed writer-in-residence at the newly-established Norwegian National Theatre in Bergen. Six years later he was made Director of the Norwegian Theatre in Kristiania (now Oslo), a post he held until 1862.

Ibsen found his years in the theatre intensely frustrating. The towns were small and the audiences parochial and frivolous-minded. His own plays at the time were chiefly historical dramas, some in verse, modelled on Shakespeare, Schiller and Hugo. In the end the Norwegian Theatre lost its audience, ran out of money, and, in 1864, after two years of poverty (aggravated by alcoholism and depression), Ibsen left Norway for Italy and Germany, countries in which he spent the next 27 years.

The first two plays Ibsen wrote in self-imposed exile, the verse dramas *Brand* (1866) and *Peer Gynt* (1867), established his reputation. With characteristic iron will, however, he immediately changed his style. He dropped verse for prose (which was more suitable, he said, for 'serious subjects'), and, from 1877 onwards, wrote no more plays on historical or folk-inspired subjects. His subsequent plays (a dozen from *The Pillars of Society*, 1879, to *When We Dead Awaken*, 1899) all dealt with contemporary social or philosophical issues, and were set among the provincial bourgeoisie. They regularly caused scandal and took time to find favour with critics and the middle-class audiences whose lives and concerns they dramatised. Other critics (notably Archer and Shaw in Britain) rallied to his cause, and by his sixties (the time of his greatest plays), he had become the grand old man not only of Scandinavian literature but of European theatre in general; the 'problem play' of which he was a pioneer has been a staple theatre genre ever since.

Ibsen returned to Norway in 1891. He wrote four more plays, but in 1901 suffered the first of a series of debilitating strokes, the last of which proved fatal.

A Doll's House: What Happens in the Play

The action takes place in the apartment of Nora and Torvald Helmer. It begins on Christmas Eve, as Nora comes home from shopping in time to decorate the tree. She and Helmer reveal their relationship in a bantering dialogue: he is possessive and treats her like a pet or a 'dolly-baby', she responds in kind. Her old schoolfriend Mrs Linde arrives, and asks Nora to beg Helmer (who has just been appointed Bank Manager) to find her a job. She, too, treats Nora as an empty-headed spendthrift, until Nora reveals that years ago, to save Helmer's life, she secretly found money to pay for a holiday in Italy. We meet Dr Rank, the Helmers' friend and regular visitor – and then we are introduced to Krogstad, from whom Nora borrowed the holiday-money. It transpires that she forged a signature to do so – and Krogstad, whom Helmer has just dismissed from the Bank, says that he will make trouble. Alone with Helmer, Nora tries to persuade him to reinstate Krogstad, but Helmer angrily refuses, saying that the man's 'crime', forging a document, makes him feel physically ill.

Act Two takes place on Christmas Day. Nora and Mrs Linde are repairing a fancy-dress which Nora is to wear at a party the following evening. Nora is on tenterhooks for the post to arrive, bringing Krogstad's letter telling Helmer the whole business of the loan. Once again Nora tries to persuade Helmer to reinstate Krogstad, without success. She nerves herself (at Mrs Linde's suggestion) to borrow money from Rank, but recoils in horror when Rank responds by declaring his long-felt love for her. Krogstad now arrives, saying that he will reveal everything unless Helmer gives him not just his old job, but a higher position. Nora answers that she will commit suicide, and Krogstad says that it will make no difference, and goes to write his letter. In despair, Nora frantically dances and sings, ostensibly practising her tarantella for the next day's party. Rank plays the piano; Helmer watches her hysteria in amazement.

Act Three takes place on the evening of Boxing Day. The Helmers are at the party, and Mrs Linde is waiting for them to come home. Krogstad arrives, and he and Mrs Linde rekindle a long-forgotten love and decide to make a new start in life, together. Krogstad goes, as Helmer and Nora return. Helmer is tipsy, but none the less Mrs Linde urges Nora to tell him everything: that is the only way they can discover the truth of their relationship. She goes, but before Nora can speak Helmer makes a clumsy, drunken pass at her. Rank now arrives, also tipsy, and announces that he is terminally ill. Helmer finds Krogstad's letter in the box behind the door, and rails at Nora for betraying his trust, being a bad mother and destroying their family life. A second letter arrives in the box – Krogstad has recanted, and returned the forged document. Helmer apologises to Nora and says that all is forgiven. To his astonishment she answers that she now sees the truth at last, about herself and about their relationship. She is not his doll, but a person in her own right, and she is leaving him to find out more of the truth about herself. Distraught, he tries to understand, tries to persuade her to stay 'on new terms' – but she has travelled too far to make such a compromise and leaves. Alone, he faces the thought that if he, too, changes, the 'miracle' may happen, and at this precise moment we hear a door slam offstage and the curtain falls.

The 'Problem' Play and the 'Well-Made' Play

The 'problem' play was a response, in mid-19th-century European theatre, to an upsurge in public discussion of 'big' social and philosophical issues. Favoured topics were the differing natures and social roles of women and men, family relationships, sexual behaviour, religion, politics and social ethics. The plays were set among ordinary, contemporary people, whose dilemmas onstage embodied the question under discussion. The 'problem' plays of some writers – for example Bjørnson in Norway, Sardou in France and Henry Arthur Jones in Britain – were often creaking and contrived: sermons or newspaper leaders disguised as art. (Shaw coined the nickname 'Sardoodledum'; Wilde memorably said, 'There are three rules for the young playwright. The first rule is not to write like Jones. The second and third rules are the same.') But in other hands, notably Ibsen's, concentration on character and on personal tragedy elevated the form: even such preachy plays as *Ghosts* or *An Enemy of the People* make their impact through the vitality of their characters and situations rather than the underlying issues they address.

Rules for the 'well-made' play were formulated in France in the early nineteenth century, and quickly spread throughout Europe. They were as strict as those Aristotle laid down for ancient tragedy. In a 'well-made' play, action should be organised in three sections: exposition of the central problem, alarms and excursions, dénouement. The plot should hinge on a secret or a dilemma which affects the main character; the audience is allowed only hints and glimpses of this as the play proceeds, and all is fully revealed only as the action moves towards dénouement. There should be reversal of fortune – 'up' in a 'well-made' farce, 'down' in a 'well-made' melodrama. And finally, settings, dialogue and behaviour should be contemporary and conventional. Tens of thousands of 'well-made' plays were written, and most are justly forgotten. (Victorian melodramas are typical examples.) But in the hands of fine writers – Dumas' *Lady of the Camellias* and Labiche's farces spring to mind, not to mention Rattigan's plays in a later age – the recipe has led to masterpieces. 'Well-made' conventions, in whole or in part, were particularly useful to writers of 'problem plays', whose effect on their audience depended, in part, on putting a spin on familiar-seeming characters and situations and on received ideas.

A Doll's House

Ibsen wrote *A Doll's House* in 1879, much of it in a holiday apartment in Amalfi; it was first published, and first performed, in December that year. From the start it attracted critical praise, and – rather more unexpectedly, perhaps, in view of the bourgeois nature of its audiences – full houses. Critics applauded its technical innovation, the way it gave tragedy a domestic setting, with no more than five main characters and an almost total absence of histrionics. It is impossible to say what drew audiences, though the fact that the 'message' of the play was much discussed, as if Ibsen had preached some kind of sermon about contemporary life, suggests that this may have been at least part of what attracted people to the theatre or made them buy the printed text (a best-seller). Possibly also the racking-up of emotional tension, which is such a feature of the action, made its impression, so that word-of-mouth soon guaranteed the play-going public a cathartic, if uncomfortable, night out.

The play was quickly taken up in Germany; it was performed in New York in 1882 and in London in 1884 – the first of Ibsen's plays to reach the US and UK, in each case initially in an adapted and somewhat emasculated form; by the mid-1890s it was part of the international repertoire, a main cause of Ibsen's worldwide reputation. The first English Helmer was Herbert Beerbohm Tree; distinguished UK Noras have included Janet Achurch, Gwen Ffrangçon-Davies, Sybil Thorndike, Flora Robson and Claire Bloom (who filmed it in 1973 with Anthony Hopkins as Helmer and Ralph Richardson as Rank); distinguished US Noras have included Beatrice Cameron (whose production caused nationwide controversy in the late 1880s), Ruth Gordon (in an adaptation by Thornton Wilder) and Jane Fonda (in a 1973 film notable for its feminist distortion of the play's message).

Right from the start, *A Doll's House* has been the prey of people who saw in it confirmation of their own prejudices about society. Calvinists in Ibsen's own country, and fundamentalist Christians of other kinds in the US, railed against its 'denunciation of marriage'; women's guilds were disgusted by its 'laxity of language', and by its depiction onstage of drunkenness, domestic wrangling and an extortioner with – horror of horrors – redeeming characteristics. The play's supporters could be equally dogmatic. In particular, from Shaw onwards (in *The Quintessence of Ibsenism*) it has regularly been claimed as a major document of women's emancipation, a trumpet-call to blow down the walls of Western, male oppression. It is still regularly overlaid with feminist interpretations, in both academic books and stage productions. Ibsen's theme *is* emancipation, but his play is, so to speak, as much peoplist as feminist. He is concerned that everyone, of either gender, should break free of conventional shackles and discover his or her own moral identity; however painful or destructive this process proves to be, Ibsen's claim is that moral truth is always better than moral lie. Nora in the play may be the most spectacular adventurer along the path to self-knowledge, but she is by no means the only one. As the action develops, all the other main characters approach a similar point of discovery in different ways and from different directions, and make their own decisions about how that discovery will affect their future actions. (Only Helmer's future action is left undecided; as the curtain falls he is at the very moment of self-discovery.)

Assertion of moral identity involves not rejection of the way other people treat us, or we them, but an examination of where we stand in relation to ourselves and others; the results of that examination may be revolt against the status quo, or acceptance, but the important thing, for Ibsen and his characters, is not the action which follows the examination but the moral purgation which precedes it. In 1880 the actress Hedwig Niemann-Raabe, about to play Nora in the German première, refused to perform the original ending on the grounds that she herself, as a mother, would never desert her children as Nora deserted hers. Ibsen, unwillingly, wrote an alternative ending (in which Helmer persuades Nora to 'think again of the little ones', and leads her to the children's door, where she collapses as the curtain falls). This subverts the entire point of the play, restores the status quo and destroys Nora's moral character – something Ibsen acknowledged by describing it as a 'barbaric outrage' on the play, and which the actress admitted by dropping the ending as soon she could, in favour of the original.

Characterisation and Irony

The role of Nora is one of the most challenging and rewarding in all Ibsen's work. In the first two acts she barely leaves the stage, and runs the gamut from simpering flirtation (ironically underscored by our knowledge that she is deliberately playing the part of a child-wife) to energetic hysteria. As the third act opens (after her strenuous dancing which ends Act Two) the actress has a respite offstage, before coming on to experience a seduction, a domestic quarrel and the total change of direction which has been implicit from the start but which now carries the action to its bleak conclusion. The volatility of the part is brilliantly offset by Helmer's rocklike steadiness: his and Nora's relationship is like a darkly tragic version of the vaudeville double act in which an anarchic, unpredictable comedian bounces off the 'straight man', whose assumption of control is constantly challenged but never abandoned. Ibsen trumps this by the ending: Helmer's collapse, in terms of what he is, is a moment of moral self-discovery as huge, and as open-ended, as anything which happens to Nora in the play.

In 19th-century Scandinavian theatre-companies of the traditional kind, there were five main performers. They took the roles, respectively, of Hero, Heroine, Confidante, Villain and 'Fifth Business'. 'Fifth Business' brought about the dénouement of the action: either the hero's or heroine's recognition that he/she was careering to self-inflicted doom, or the revelation or incident which brought destruction or salvation from outside the characters. (If coincidence brought happiness at the end of a melodrama, that coincidence was manipulated by 'Fifth Business'.) In *A Doll's House* Ibsen uses all five of the standard categories, but all – and especially 'Fifth Business' – are fluid. Save in numbers of lines (not, of course, the least consideration in some acting-companies then, and now) Helmer is not exclusively the hero; Nora is not solely the heroine; the roles of villain, confidante and 'Fifth Business' circulate among the other characters. In particular, characters we initially think are 'good' are shown to have 'bad' qualities and motives, and vice versa. Mrs Linde's motives seem confused and opaque, until she reveals that everything she does is the result of a process of self-examination (long past) similar to the one which Nora is currently undergoing and which Mrs Linde both encourages and compels. Krogstad seems a heartless villain until – melodramatically – he is 'redeemed' in Act Three and shown to have been acting, however wickedly, out of morally understandable motives. (This revelation is one of the least 'prepared' moments in the play, hardly forseeable from what we learn of Krogstad's character and history in earlier scenes.) Rank is that favourite Ibsen secondary character, the apparently amoral, sardonic bystander – but in this play, he has a 'terrible secret' which explains, if it never excuses, his outlook on life, and which makes him a fascinating foil for Helmer's apparently flawless rectitude.

If the details of Ibsen's plot are occasionally melodramatic, his over-riding theme (moral self-examination) removes the play entirely from mechanistic cliché. The blurring and ambiguity of character (never features of melodrama) allow him a greater degree of irony than in any of his other plays. Almost from the beginning of Act One, we know that Nora is nursing a terrible secret, and that her behaviour with Helmer is desperate play-acting – a knowledge which is itself ironically undercut because she herself half believes in, and certainly assents in, the 'reality' of the part she plays. We know that Helmer's unquestioning self-certainty is a house of cards, that Rank's apparent bonhomie will have its darker side, that Mrs Linde has some hidden purpose in coming back to town. Above all, and although we know that Krogstad will not easily surrender his hold on Nora, we still know less than he does about his motives and his intentions, matters which are them-selves to change in view of factors of which he himself is unaware. The irony in *A Doll's House* is on many interlocking levels, and it shifts as the action develops, creating and enhancing the play's extraordinary psychological tension. Consistently, we are less intrigued by the characters' motives and nature than by what they know, and by how soon and in what way they will find out more than they know. In his third act, Ibsen exploits this state of affairs between dramatist and audience to give his moral theme more power. Nora's (apparent) volte-face is shocking because it is (apparently) unexpected; the irony is that it is inevitable, and predictable, almost from the opening line.

Language

Ibsen was concerned, in his prose plays, to write the kind of language which ordinary people spoke in everyday life. (He objected strongly to 'literary' translations, insisting that the plays should be rendered as far as possible in the vernacular of the place and period in which they were to be performed.) *A Doll's House* is remarkable for the ordinariness of its language. There are so few literary or histrionic flights that the simplest of metaphors (the singing bird), the plainest of images (Krogstad's vision of the 'deep dark depths' into which Nora may throw herself) or the briefest of fancies (Nora's and Rank's flirtatious – desperately flirtatious – discussion of the foie gras and oysters which may have comprised Rank's father's dissipation) all impact like bombs. Because voices are seldom raised, Nora's hysteria at the end of the second act, and Helmer's fury after he reads the letter, seem almost unbearably violent. Helmer's attempted seduction, half a dozen lines of suggestion and murmur, shrieks, in context, like a scream in church. (This passage was one of those which provoked outrage among Ibsen's more staid contemporaries.) The play's impression of frankness comes not from the words spoken, but from the feeling that we are walking on the characters' very nerve-ends, on the raw flesh of their relationships. When the characters in Osborne's *Look Back in Anger* use baby-talk, it repels because we know they hate it; when Nora and Helmer use it, our horror is intensified because we know that they both believe, or wish, that it may be 'real'. Without ever being overt, the play is consistently frank about matters which had never before been so laid out for public inspection. Before the spectators' eyes, intimacy is violated – not the intimacy of Man and Woman in general, but the intimacy of one particular woman and one particular man – and this is why, even today, when Ibsen's 'messages' have long been part of our emotional, psychological and dramatic baggage, *A Doll's House* can still seem one of his most uncomfortable, most shocking and most moving plays.

Stage Directions

To modern eyes, Ibsen's plays can seem cluttered with unnecessarily explicit stage-directions. In particular, his instructions to the actors about how to deliver the lines can seem both pedantic and fustian. Modern conventions, we might argue, are different; we play by our own rules. But it seems at least plausible that Ibsen, so scrupulous about every other kind of artistic effect, might have organised the emotional blocking of each scene with as much care as he did everything else. What we have, in short, may be analogous less to the stage-directions in an 'acting edition' than to the instructions for performing-nuance which composers write on music. For this reason, the present translation retains all original directions, whether they look over-explicit or not.

Kenneth McLeish, 1994

For Further Reading

Michael Meyer, *Henrik Ibsen* (3 vols, 1967-71; 1 vol, 1992) is a
lively biography, plump with quotations from letters, reviews
and other documents, and excellent on the theatrical and
political background to Ibsen's life. Its only defect – somewhat
heavy-handed literary criticism – is offset by John Northam,
Ibsen: a Critical Study (1973): a scholarly but readable discussion
of themes and techniques in the prose plays. The most
recommendable book on Ibsen is the oldest of the three:
George Bernard Shaw, *The Quintessence of Ibsenism* (1891).
Written by one of Ibsen's first European devotees (anxious to
give the master a place in serious drama analogous to
Wagner's in music), it balances gush and fervour with
remarkably clear-headed intellectual and technical discussion
of Ibsen's ideas and the ways in which he realises them. Shaw
is wrong about the 'message' of *A Doll's House*, crediting Ibsen
with Shaw's own obsessions about society; but it is excellent
about how the play is constructed, about how a dramatist
actually goes to work.

Ibsen: Key Dates

1828	Born (to well-to-do, bourgeois parents)
1832	Father bankrupt
1843	Apprenticed to an apothecary
1850	Fails university entrance exam; writes first play (*Catiline*)
1851	Playwright-in-residence at National Theatre in Bergen
1857	Appointed Director of Norwegian Theatre, Kristiania
1862	Theatre closed down
1864	Moves to Rome
1866	*Brand*
1867	*Peer Gynt*
1868	Moves to Dresden
1869	*The League of Youth*
1873	*Emperor and Galilean*
1877	*Pillars of the Community*
1879	*A Doll's House*
1881	Returns to Rome; *Ghosts*
1882	*An Enemy of the People*
1884	*The Wild Duck*
1885	Moves to Munich; spends summer in Norway (first visit since 1864)
1886	*Rosmersholm*
1888	*The Lady from the Sea*
1890	*Hedda Gabler*

Characters

HELMER

NORA, his wife

DOCTOR RANK

MRS LINDE

KROGSTAD

Helmer's three young CHILDREN

ANNE-MARIE, their nanny

MAID

PORTER

The action takes place in Helmer's apartment.

A DOLL'S HOUSE

Act One

Room in HELMER's *apartment. The decoration is not extravagant, but comfortable and stylish. Back right, door to the hall; back left, door to* HELMER's *study. Between the doors, a piano. Centre left, a door, and beyond it a window; beside the window a round table, easy chairs and a small sofa. Upstage right, a door, and below it a stove, two easy chairs and a rocking chair. Between the door and the stove, a side-table. Engravings on the walls. A cabinet filled with china and other small objects; a small bookcase with expensively-bound books. Carpet on the floor, fire in the stove. Winter.*

A bell rings in the hall, off, and soon afterwards we hear the door being opened. Enter NORA. *She is happy, humming a tune. She is dressed in outdoor clothes, and carries a number of parcels, which she puts down on the table, right. She leaves the hall door open, and through it can be seen a* PORTER, *carrying a Christmas tree and a basket. He gives them to the* CHAMBERMAID, *who has opened the door.*

NORA. Make sure you hide it, Helene. The children mustn't see it till tonight, after it's trimmed. (*To the* PORTER, *taking out her purse.*) How much is that?

PORTER. Fifty øre.

NORA. Keep the change.

The PORTER *thanks her and goes.* NORA *closes the door. She takes off her coat, laughing to herself. She takes a bag of macaroons from her pocket and eats two of them. Then she goes cautiously and listens at* HELMER's *door.*

He is home.

Still humming, she goes to the table right, and starts opening the parcels.

HELMER (*off*). Is that my little songbird piping away out there?

NORA. Yes it is.

HELMER (*off*). Is that my little squirrel rustling?

NORA. Yes.

HELMER (*off*). When did squirrelkin come home?

NORA. Just now.

She puts the macaroons in her pocket and wipes her mouth.

Come out here, Torvald, and see what I bought.

HELMER (*off*). Just a moment.

After a short pause, he opens the door and looks in, pen in hand.

Did you say bought? All those? Has my little songbird been spending all my money again?

NORA. Oh Torvald, this year we can let ourselves go a little. It's the first Christmas we don't have to scrimp and save.

HELMER. That doesn't mean we've money to burn.

NORA. Can't we burn just a little? A tiny little? Now you're getting such a big pay-packet, pennies and pennies and pennies.

HELMER. After January the first. And even then we won't see the money till the end of the first quarter.

NORA. Oh fiddle, we can borrow till then.

HELMER. Nora!

He takes her playfully by the ear.

What a little featherbrain it is! I borrow a thousand kroner today, you spend it all by Christmas, and on New Year's Eve a tile falls on my head and kills me –

NORA (*hand to mouth*). Don't say that.

HELMER. But suppose it did?

NORA. If it did, why would I care if I still owed people money?

HELMER. But what about them? The people I borrowed it from?

NORA. Who cares about them? I don't even know their names.

HELMER. Just like a woman! But seriously, you know what I think. No borrowing. No debt. When a household relies on debt, it's slavery, it's vile. We've struggled this far without, the two of us – and we'll struggle on for a few more weeks, till we don't have to struggle any more.

NORA (*crossing to the stove*). Yes, Torvald.

HELMER (*following*). There, there. Poor little songbird, drooping her wings? Little squirrel, making sulky faces?

He takes out his wallet.

Nora, what have I here?

NORA (*turning quickly*). Pennies!

HELMER. Look. (*Giving her money.*) Heavens, d'you think I don't know what it costs at Christmastime?

NORA (*counting*). Ten, twenty, thirty, forty. Oh thankyou, Torvald, thankyou. Now I'll manage.

HELMER. You must.

NORA. I will. Now come here, and see what I've bought. Bargains! A new outfit for Ivar, and a little sword. A horse and a trumpet for Bob. A dolly and a dolly's bed for Emmy. Nothing expensive: they'll soon be broken, anyway. Dress-lengths and hankies for the maids. Old Anne-Marie should really have something better.

HELMER. What's in this one?

NORA (*with a shriek*). No, Torvald. Not till tonight!

HELMER. And what about my own little spendthrift? What would she like, herself?

NORA. Oh fiddle. Me? I don't want anything.

HELMER. Of course you do. Tell me some little thing you'd like more than all the world.

NORA. I really don't . . . Unless . . . Torvald . . .

HELMER. Yes?

NORA (*playing with his buttons, not looking at him*). If you really want to give me something, you could . . . you could . . .

HELMER. Out with it.

NORA (*blurting it*). Give me some pennies of my own. Just what you can spare. I could keep them till I really wanted something . . .

HELMER. Oh, Nora –

NORA. Please, Torvald, please. I'll wrap them in pretty paper and hang them on the tree. They'll be so pretty.

HELMER. What do they call little birds that are always wasting money?

NORA. Featherbrains. I know. But why don't we try it, Torvald, try it? Give me time to think what I'd really like? It would be a good idea.

HELMER (*smiling*). Of course it would – if you really did manage to save it, to spend on yourself. But it'll just go into the housekeeping, you'll spend it on this or that, and I'll end up forking out again.

NORA. No, Torvald.

HELMER. Darling Nora, yes.

He puts his arm round her waist.

What a sweet little featherbrain it is. But it swallows up so many pennies. It costs a lot of pennies, to keep a little featherbrain.

NORA. Don't be horrid. I do save, all I can.

HELMER (*with a laugh*). All you can. That's right. The whole trouble is, you can't.

NORA (*smiling gently and playfully*). Oh Torvald, songbirds, squirrels, you know how we spend and spend.

HELMER. What a funny little thing it is. Daddy's daughter. A thousand little ways of wheedling pennies – and as soon as you've got them, they melt in your hands. You never know where they've gone. It's in the blood, little Nora, it's inherited.

NORA. I wish I'd inherited some of Daddy's other qualities.

HELMER. I wouldn't have you any different. Dear little bird, little darling. But what is it? There's something, isn't there? There is.

NORA. What?

HELMER. Look at me.

NORA (*looking at him*). There.

HELMER (*wagging his finger*). Was little Miss Sweet-tooth naughty in town today?

NORA. What d'you mean?

HELMER. Did she visit the sweetie-shop?

NORA. No, Torvald. I promise.

HELMER. She's not been nibbling?

NORA. No. No.

HELMER. Not one tiny macaroon?

NORA. Torvald, I swear –

HELMER. It's all right. I was only joking.

NORA (*crossing to the table right*). You told me not to. You don't really think I'd – ?

HELMER. Of course not. You promised.

He goes to her.

Darling Nora, keep all your Christmas secrets to yourself.

They'll all come out this evening, when we light the tree.

NORA. Did you remember to invite Dr Rank?

HELMER. There's no need: he'll eat with us, goes without saying. I'll ask him when he comes this morning. I've ordered good wine. Nora, you can't imagine how much I'm looking forward to this evening.

NORA. So am I. Oh Torvald, what fun the children will have!

HELMER. A secure job, a good income – isn't it wonderful?

NORA. Wonderful.

HELMER. Remember last Christmas? How you shut yourself in here evening after evening for three whole weeks, making tree-decorations and all the other surprises? The dullest three weeks I've ever spent.

NORA. I wasn't bored.

HELMER (*smiling*). It's not as if anything much came of it, Nora.

NORA. Don't be horrid. How could I guess that the cat would get in and tear everything to bits?

HELMER. There, there, of course you couldn't. You wanted to please us all, that was the main thing. But thank goodness, even so, that those hard times are past us now.

NORA. It's really wonderful.

HELMER. No more Torvald sitting all alone and bored. No more Nora wearing out her lovely eyes, her pretty little fingers –

NORA (*clapping her hands*). No, Torvald, never again! (*taking his arm.*) Now, shall I tell you what we ought to do? As soon as Christmas is over –

Ring at the bell, off.

A visitor.

She begins tidying the room.

What a nuisance.

HELMER. I'm not at home.

MAID (*at the door*). There's a lady, madam . . . a stranger.

NORA. Show her in.

MAID (*to* HELMER). The doctor's here too.

HELMER. In the study?

MAID. Yes, sir.

HELMER *goes into the study. The* MAID *shows in* MRS LINDE, *who is wearing travelling clothes, and shuts the door after her.*

MRS LINDE (*timidly, rather ill-at-ease*). Good morning, Nora.

NORA (*hesitantly*). Good morning.

MRS LINDE. You don't recognise me.

NORA. No, I . . . just a minute . . . (*suddenly.*) Kristine!

MRS LINDE. That's right.

NORA. Kristine! To think I didn't recognise you. (*more subdued.*) You've changed, Kristine.

MRS LINDE. Nine, ten years –

NORA. Is it really so long? I suppose it is. I've been so happy these last eight years. And now you've come back to town. Such a long journey, in winter too. Aren't you brave?

MRS LINDE. I came on the steamer this morning.

NORA. Just in time for Christmas. What a lovely surprise! What a time we'll have. Take your coat off. You can't be cold. (*helping her.*) There. Let's be cosy, by the stove. This armchair. I'll sit in the rocking chair. (*taking her hands.*) That's better. Now you're like you always were. It was just that first moment. You're paler, Kristine, thinner.

MRS LINDE. Older.

NORA. A tiny bit.

Suddenly she breaks off, and speaks seriously.

How thoughtless of me, sitting here chattering. Kristine, darling, I'm sorry.

MRS LINDE. What d'you mean?

NORA (*with sympathy*). Dear Kristine, you lost your husband.

MRS LINDE. Three years ago.

NORA. I read it in the paper. I did mean to write. I thought about it, often. But I kept putting it off . . . there was always something . . .

MRS LINDE. Don't worry.

NORA. It was horrid of me. Poor Kristine. Did he leave you enough to live on?

MRS LINDE. No.

NORA. You've children?

MRS LINDE. No.

NORA. You've nothing?

MRS LINDE. Not even sad memories.

NORA (*looking at her in amazement*). But surely – ?

MRS LINDE (*smiling sadly, stroking her hair*). It happens, Nora.

NORA. Completely alone. That must be awful. I've got three beautiful children. They aren't here now, they're out with Nanny. But tell me everything.

MRS LINDE. No, no, you first.

NORA. No, you. Today I won't be selfish. I'll put you first. But there is just one thing – d'you know what a stroke of luck we've had?

MRS LINDE. What is it?

NORA. They've made my husband manager. At the Bank!

MRS LINDE. That's wonderful.

NORA. Unbelievable. He was a lawyer. But that's not secure, especially if you won't take on cases for people you don't approve of. Torvald never would, and of course I agree with him. But now! Imagine! He starts in the New Year. A big salary and lots of bonuses. Our lives'll be so different. We'll be able to do anything we want. Oh Kristine, I'm so relieved, so happy. To have no more worries, all one needs. Isn't it wonderful?

MRS LINDE. Wonderful, yes, to have all one needs.

NORA. Not just all one needs, but lots of money, lots.

MRS LINDE (*lightly*). Nora, Nora, have you still not grown up? You were an extravagant little thing at school.

NORA (*with a light laugh*). That's just what Torvald calls me. (*wagging a finger*.) 'Nora, Nora' – she's not all featherbrain. Not all you both think. We've never had the money for me to waste. We've had to work, both of us.

MRS LINDE. You, as well?

NORA. Odds and ends. Sewing, embroidery, things like that. (*in a low voice*.) And other things too. You know Torvald set up on his own when we got married? He'd no prospects at the office, and he had to earn more money. In the first year, he overworked terribly. It was because of the money. He worked every hour there was. It was too much for him. He had a breakdown, and the doctors said he had to get away, go South.

MRS LINDE. You went to Italy, didn't you? A year in Italy.

NORA. It was hard to get away. It was just after Ivar was born. But we simply had to. It was wonderful, Kristine, and it saved Torvald's life. The only thing was, it cost a fortune.

MRS LINDE. I can imagine.

NORA. Four thousand, eight hundred kroner. A fortune.

MRS LINDE. You were lucky to have it, just when you needed it.

NORA. Ah well, it came from Daddy.

MRS LINDE. I remember, your father died about that time.

NORA. Can you imagine, I couldn't go and look after him? I
    was expecting Ivar, any day. Torvald was really ill. Poor,
    darling Daddy. I never saw him again, Kristine. It was the
    worst time of my whole married life.

MRS LINDE. I know how fond you were of him. But then
    you all went to Italy.

NORA. We had the money then, and the doctors insisted. So
    we went, a month later.

MRS LINDE. And your husband recovered?

NORA. Oh yes, yes.

MRS LINDE. But . . . the doctor?

NORA. Pardon?

MRS LINDE. I thought the maid said that was the doctor,
    that man who arrived at the same time I did.

NORA. Oh, Dr Rank. It's not because anyone's ill. An old
    friend – he comes every day. No, since Italy, Torvald
    hasn't had a moment's illness. The children are fine, and so
    am I.

She jumps up and claps her hands.

Kristine, it's all so wonderful. We're so happy, so lucky.
Oh . . . how awful of me. Talking of nothing but myself.

She sits on a stool beside her, and rests her arms on her knee.

Don't be cross. Is it really true, you didn't love him, your
husband? Why ever did you marry him?

MRS LINDE. My mother was still alive: bedridden, helpless.
    I'd two younger brothers to look after. When he proposed,

how could I not accept?

NORA. He'd money too, hadn't he?

MRS LINDE. Then, he did. I think. But his business was
shaky. After he died, it collapsed entirely. There was
nothing left.

NORA. So how did you – ?

MRS LINDE. Whatever I could find. A shop . . . a little
school . . . It's been endless hard work, these last three
years. I haven't had a moment. But now it's finished. My
mother's passed on, needs nothing more. The boys have
jobs, they don't need me either –

NORA. You must feel so relieved!

MRS LINDE. No, empty. No one left to live for.

She gets up, in distress.

I couldn't bear it any longer, life in that backwater. Better
to find something here, to occupy me, to fill my mind. If I
could get a job, some kind of office job –

NORA. But that'll be exhausting, Kristine. Draining. You
look worn out. Why don't you go away somewhere, have a
holiday?

MRS LINDE (*crossing to the window*). Dear Nora, I've no
Daddy to pay the bills.

NORA (*getting up*). Don't be cross with me.

MRS LINDE (*going to her*). Nora, don't you be cross. The
worst thing about a situation like mine is that it makes you
hard. No one else to work for; always out for yourself;

survival, it makes you selfish. You won't believe this: when
you told me how well things were going for you, I was
delighted – not for you, for me.

NORA. Pardon? Oh. If Torvald did something for you . . .

MRS LINDE. Yes.

NORA. Of course he will, Kristine. Leave it to me. I'll see to
it. I'll find a way. Put him in a good mood. I'd love to help
you.

MRS LINDE. You're so kind. To be so eager to help me.
Especially you, when you've so little idea how difficult life
can be.

NORA. Me – ?

MRS LINDE (*with a smile*). Sewing, embroidering . . . Nora,
you're a babe in arms.

NORA (*moving away, with a toss of the head*). Don't be so snooty.

MRS LINDE. What d'you mean?

NORA. You're all the same. None of you think I can manage
anything . . . serious.

MRS LINDE. No, no.

NORA. You think I don't know how hard life is.

MRS LINDE. But you've just told me yourself. Your
problems.

NORA. Fiddle. They were nothing. (*quietly.*) I haven't told you
the real one.

MRS LINDE. What real one?

NORA. You don't take me seriously. You should. Aren't you proud of all you did, all that hard work for your mother?

MRS LINDE. I take everyone seriously. Of course I'm proud, I made my mother's last months a little easier.

NORA. And your brothers – you're proud of what you did for them.

MRS LINDE. I've a right to be.

NORA. Of course you have. And so do I. I've a right to be proud too.

MRS LINDE. Why? What d'you mean?

NORA. Sh! Torvald must never hear. He mustn't ever – no one in the world must ever know, except you, Kristine.

MRS LINDE. Know what?

NORA. Come over here.

She pulls her to the sofa and sits beside her.

I *have* got something to be proud of. The person who saved Torvald's life – it was me.

MRS LINDE. Saved his life? How?

NORA. The trip to Italy. I told you. If he hadn't gone –

MRS LINDE. But your father –

NORA (*smiling*). That's what everyone thought. Torvald . . . everyone.

MRS LINDE. But –

NORA. We didn't have a penny from Daddy. I paid. I got the money.

MRS LINDE. All of it?

NORA. Four thousand, eight hundred kroner.

MRS LINDE. Nora, how? Did you win the Lottery?

NORA (*scornfully*). The Lottery! Pff! *That* wouldn't have been clever.

MRS LINDE. How did you get it, then?

NORA (*smiling mysteriously, humming*). Hm, hm, hm.

MRS LINDE. You didn't – *borrow* it?

NORA. Why not?

MRS LINDE. A wife can't borrow without her husband's permission.

NORA (*tossing her head*). Unless she knows about business . . . knows her way around.

MRS LINDE. I don't understand.

NORA. Never mind. I didn't say I *did* borrow it. There are plenty of other ways.

She stretches out on the sofa.

Perhaps it was one of my admirers. I'm such a pretty little thing . . .

MRS LINDE. You are silly.

NORA. And you're nosy.

MRS LINDE. Nora. Are you sure you haven't done something . . . rash?

NORA (*sitting up straight*). Saving my husband's life?

MRS LINDE. I mean rash, if he didn't know – ?

NORA. That's the whole point. He wasn't to know. Don't you understand? He was never to know how ill he was. The doctors came to me, to me, and told me his life depended on it. Time in the South, in the sun. D'you think I didn't try to wheedle him? I told him it was for me, how lovely it would be to go abroad, like other young wives. I begged, I cried. I told him to think of my condition, he had to be kind to me, humour me. I hinted that he took out a loan. Kristine, he almost lost his temper. He said I was featherbrained, and his duty as a husband was not to indulge my . . . my little whims, he called them. Right, right, I thought. If you won't save yourself . . . So I . . . found a way myself.

MRS LINDE. Torvald never knew the money wasn't from your father?

NORA. Of course not. Daddy died about that time. I'd wanted to tell him, to ask him to help. But first he was too ill, then it was too late.

MRS LINDE. And you've never told your husband?

NORA. For heaven's sake! When he thinks the way he does. In any case, Torvald, a man, proud to be a man – how d'you imagine he'd feel if he knew he owed anything to me? It would break us apart. Our lovely home, our happiness – all gone.

MRS LINDE. You won't ever tell him?

NORA (*thoughtfully, with a light smile*). One day. Perhaps. When I'm not quite such a pretty little thing. Don't laugh. I mean when Torvald isn't as smitten as he is now, when he's tired

of me dancing, reciting, dressing up. Then I may need
something in reserve. (*Abruptly*.) Da, da, da. It'll never
happen. Well, Kristine? What d'you think of my great big
secret? D'you still think I'm silly? No cares in all the world?
Don't think it's been easy, meeting the payments on time,
each time. Quarterly accounts, instalments – I can tell you
all about that sort of thing. Keeping up with them's not
easy. I've saved a little bit here, a little bit there. Not much
from the housekeeping, because of Torvald's position. The
children couldn't go without nice clothes. Every penny he
gave me for my little darlings, I spent on them.

MRS LINDE. Oh, Nora! It came out of your own allowance?

NORA. What else? That was mine to do as I liked with.
Every time Torvald gave me money for clothes, I put half
of it away. I bought the simplest, cheapest things. Thank
heavens everything looks good on me: Torvald never
noticed. But it was hard, Kristine, often. It's nice to wear
nice clothes. Don't you think?

KRISTINE. Oh . . . yes, yes.

NORA. Fortunately there were other things I could do. Last
winter I was lucky: I got a lot of copying. I locked myself in
every evening and sat and wrote, into the small hours. It
was exhausting. But it was thrilling too, to be sitting there
working, earning money. Almost like a man.

MRS LINDE. How much have you paid back?

NORA. I really don't know. Business: it's hard to keep track
of. All I know is, I paid every penny I could scrape
together. The number of times I didn't know *how* I'd
manage! (*smiling.*) When that happened, I used to sit and

daydream. A rich old man was head over heels in love with
me –

MRS LINDE. What? Who?

NORA. Sh! He died, and when they read his will, there it was
in capital letters: ALL MY CASH TO BE PAID OVER INSTANTER
TO THAT DELIGHTFUL NORA HELMER.

MRS LINDE. Nora! Who on Earth was it?

NORA. Heavens, can't you guess? He didn't exist, he just
came into my head every time I sat here thinking how to
get some money. It doesn't matter now, anyway. The silly
old nuisance can stay away; I don't need him and I don't
need his will. I'm free of it! (*jumping up.*) Free, Kristine, free
of it! I can play with the children . . . make the house
pretty, make everything the way Torvald likes it. It'll soon
be spring, the wide blue sky. We could have a holiday . . .
the seaside. Free of it! I'm so happy, so happy.

A bell rings, off.

MRS LINDE (*getting up*). I'd better go.

NORA. No, stay. It'll be for Torvald.

MAID (*in the doorway from the hall*). Excuse me, madam. There's
a gentleman here to see the master.

NORA. To see the Bank Manager.

MAID. Yes, madam. But I didn't know if . . . Dr Rank's still
there.

NORA. Who is the gentleman?

KROGSTAD (*at the door*). Me, Mrs Helmer.

*MRS LINDE starts, then goes over to the window. NORA goes
closer to KROGSTAD, and speaks in a low, strained voice.*

NORA. You. What is it? What d'you want with my husband?

KROGSTAD. Bank business. I work for the Bank, very
junior. Your husband's the new manager, and so –

NORA. So it's –

KROGSTAD. Business, Mrs Helmer. Nothing else.

NORA. Please go in, then. Into the study.

*She inclines her head casually, closes the hall door, then goes and
starts making up the stove.*

MRS LINDE. Nora, who was that?

NORA. Krogstad. Used to be a lawyer.

MRS LINDE. Oh yes.

NORA. You knew him?

MRS LINDE. A long time ago. He was a solicitor's clerk.

NORA. That's right.

MRS LINDE. How he's changed..

NORA. Unhappy marriage.

MRS LINDE. Didn't his wife die? Isn't he a widower?

NORA. With a houseful of children. There, that's better.

She shuts the stove and moves the rocking chair to one side.

MRS LINDE. What does he do now?

NORA. I don't know. Don't let's talk about business: it's boring.

DR RANK *comes out from* HELMER*'s study.*

RANK (*at the door*). No, no, my dear chap. I'll get out of your way. I'll talk to Nora.

He shuts the door, then notices MRS LINDE.

Oh, excuse me. Company here as well.

NORA. It's all right. (*introducing them.*) Dr Rank, Mrs Linde.

RANK. Dear lady. We often hear your name in this house. Didn't I pass you on the stairs just now?

MRS LINDE. I go slowly; I find stairs hard.

RANK. You're not well?

MRS LINDE. Overworked.

RANK. Ah. So you came to town for our . . . distractions?

MRS LINDE. To find work.

RANK. Is that the best cure for overwork?

MRS LINDE. One has to live.

RANK. Yes. So they say.

NORA. Oh Doctor . . . you know *you* want to live.

RANK. Most certainly. However dreadful I feel, I want to prolong the agony as long as possible. My patients all feel the same way. Not to mention those who are morally sick – one of whom, very far gone, is with Helmer even as we speak.

MRS LINDE (*distressed*). Oh.

NORA. Whoever do you mean?

RANK. Krogstad, his name is. An ex-lawyer. No one you
know. Totally depraved. But even he was prattling on
about how he had to *live.*

NORA. Why did he want to talk to Torvald?

RANK. Something about the Bank.

NORA. I didn't know Krog – Mr Krogstad – was connected
with the Bank.

RANK. He's got some sort of position there. (*to* MRS
LINDE.) I don't know if it's the same where you are. Some
people go round sniffing out weakness . . . and as soon as
they find it, they back the person concerned into a corner,
a . . . profitable corner. No escape. If you're strong, they
leave you alone.

MRS LINDE. You don't need curing unless you're sick.

RANK (*shrugging*). – and that makes all society a nursing
home.

NORA *has been absorbed in her own thoughts; now she smothers a
laugh and claps her hands.*

How else would you describe society?

NORA. What do I care about silly old society? I'm laughing
at something else. Dr Rank, it's true, isn't it? Everyone who
works at the Bank has to answer to Torvald now?

RANK. You find that funny?

NORA (*smiling, humming*). No, no. (*pacing.*) It's just odd to think
that we – that Torvald has power over so many people.
(*taking the sweet packet from her pocket.*) Dr Rank, a macaroon?

RANK. I thought they were forbidden.

NORA. Kristine gave me these.

MRS LINDE. What?

NORA. It's all right. You didn't know Torvald had forbidden them. He thinks they'll ruin my teeth. Fiddle! Just once in a while. Dr Rank, don't you agree? Have one.

She puts a macaroon in his mouth.

You too, Kristine. I'll have one too. Just a little one. Perhaps two. (*pacing again.*) I'm really so happy. There's only one thing left –

RANK. What's that?

NORA. I'd like to say something straight out. Something to Torvald.

RANK. Why don't you, then?

NORA. I daren't. It's too terrible.

MRS LINDE. Terrible?

RANK. If it's terrible, you'd better not. Say it to us, if you like. What is it you'd say to Helmer, if he was here?

NORA. I'd say – Good God!

RANK. Tut, tut.

MRS LINDE. Don't be silly, Nora.

RANK. He *is* here. Say it.

NORA (*hiding the macaroon-packet*). Sh!

HELMER *comes out of his study, with his coat over his arm and his hat in his hand.* NORA *runs to him.*

Torvald, darling, did you get rid of him?

HELMER. Yes, he's gone.

NORA. Let me introduce you. This is Kristine. She's come to town.

HELMER. I'm sorry . . . Kristine . . . ?

NORA. Mrs Linde, darling. Kristine Linde.

HELMER. Oh yes. One of Nora's schoolfriends?

MRS LINDE. We knew each other once.

NORA. Just imagine, she's come all this way just to talk to you.

HELMER. Pardon?

MRS LINDE. No, no, I –

NORA. Kristine's a genius at book-keeping. All she needs is the right man to work for, someone who'll show her even more than she knows already.

HELMER. Very commendable, Mrs Linde.

NORA. So of course, as soon as she heard that you were the new Bank Manager – they sent a telegram – she came here as fast as she could . . . Torvald, won't you find her something? For my sake?

HELMER. It's not a bad idea. Madam, are you a widow?

MRS LINDE. Yes.

HELMER. You've book-keeping experience?

MRS LINDE. A bit.

HELMER. I may well have something –

NORA (*clapping her hands*). See? See?

HELMER. In fact, Mrs Linde, you could hardly have come at a better time.

MRS LINDE. How can I ever thank you?

HELMER. Oh, that's all right. (*putting on his coat.*) But for the moment, if you'll excuse me . . .

RANK. Wait. I'll go with you.

He takes his fur coat and warms it at the stove.

NORA. Don't be too long, darling.

HELMER. An hour, no more.

NORA. Are you going too, Kristine?

MRS LINDE (*putting on her coat*). I need to find a room.

HELMER. We'll walk along together.

NORA (*helping her*). It's a shame we're so cramped here. We just can't –

MRS LINDE. No, no. Bye-bye, Nora – and thanks.

NORA. Till tomorrow. Yes, come tomorrow. You too, Dr Rank. What – if you're well enough? Of course you will be. Wrap up well.

They go towards the hall, all talking. Children's voices on the stairs outside.

They're here! They're here!

She runs to open the door. ANNE-MARIE, *the nanny, comes in with the* CHILDREN.

Come in. Come in.

She bends to kiss them.

Darlings. Dear little darlings. Kristine, aren't they darlings?

RANK. Let's get out of the draught.

HELMER. This way, Mrs Linde. This'll soon be no place to be, except for mothers.

He, RANK *and* MRS LINDE *go downstairs.* ANNE-MARIE *and the* CHILDREN *come into the room, followed by* NORA, *who closes the hall door. The* CHILDREN *chatter to her during what follows.*

NORA. Haven't you had fun? Such rosy cheeks. Like little red apples. Have you had a lovely time? What, both of them? Emmy *and* Bob? Both on the sledge at once. And you pulled them, Ivar? What a clever boy. Let me hold her a moment, Anne-Marie. My own little dolly-baby.

She takes the smallest CHILD *and dances with her in her arms.*

Yes, Bob. I'll dance with you too. Did you? Snowballs? I wish I'd been there. It's all right, Anne-Marie, I'll take their coats off. No, no, I enjoy it. You go in. You look frozen. There's coffee on the stove.

ANNE-MARIE *goes into the room left.* NORA *helps the* CHILDREN *out of their coats and scatters them about, as the* CHILDREN *all talk to her at once.*

A big dog? Ran after you? Of course it didn't bite. Dogs don't bite dear little dolly-babies. Don't touch those, Ivar.

Wait and see. A surprise. Let's play a game. Let's play . . .
hide and seek. Bob hide first. What? Mummy hide first? All
right. You try to find me.

She and the CHILDREN *play, laughing and shouting, running in
and out of the room on the right. Eventually* NORA *hides under the
table. The* CHILDREN *run in, but can't find her, till they hear her
smothered laughter, lift up the ends of the tablecloth and see her.
Shrieks of delight. She crawls out, pretending to frighten them. Louder
shrieks. Meanwhile someone has knocked at the hall door, unheard.
The door is half opened, and* KROGSTAD *appears. He waits in
the doorway. The game continues.*

KROGSTAD. Excuse me. Mrs Helmer.

NORA gives a stifled cry, and gets to her knees.

NORA. Ah! What is it?

KROGSTAD. I'm sorry. The door was on the latch . . .

NORA (*getting up*). Mr Krogstad, my husband's out.

KROGSTAD. I know.

NORA. Then . . . what is it?

KROGSTAD. It's you I want to talk to.

NORA. Me? (*gently, to the* CHILDREN.) Go in there, to Anne-
Marie. What? No, the man won't hurt Mummy. When
he's gone, we'll have another game.

*She takes the children into the room left, and shuts the door behind
them. She is uneasy, and speaks tightly.*

You want to talk to me?

KROGSTAD. Yes.

NORA. It's not the first of the month.

KROGSTAD. It's Christmas Eve. And what sort of Christmas Day you have, depends on you.

NORA. I can't do anything today.

KROGSTAD. It's not that. Later. It's something else. You have got a moment – ?

NORA. Yes. Of course. I . . . Yes.

KROGSTAD. I was in Olsen's Restaurant and saw your husband in the street.

NORA. Yes?

KROGSTAD. With a woman.

NORA. What of it?

KROGSTAD. Pardon me for asking, but was that Mrs Linde?

NORA. Yes.

KROGSTAD. Just arrived?

NORA. Today.

KROGSTAD. A friend of yours?

NORA. I don't –

KROGSTAD. Mine too. Once.

NORA. I know.

KROGSTAD. Ah. Well, I'll ask straight out: has Mrs Linde been given a job in the Bank?

NORA. Mr Krogstad, you shouldn't ask me that. An

employee. But since you have . . . Yes, Mrs Linde has been
given a job. On my recommendation. Satisfied?

KROGSTAD. I thought she had.

NORA (*pacing*). One isn't without influence. Just because one's
a woman. And employees, Mr Krogstad, people in
positions of dependence, should be careful not to annoy
people who, people who . . .

KROGSTAD. Have influence?

NORA. Exactly.

KROGSTAD (*changed tone*). Mrs Helmer, you'll oblige me by
putting your influence to work for me.

NORA. What d'you mean?

KROGSTAD. You'll oblige me by making sure that I keep
my . . . position of dependence in the Bank.

NORA. Is someone taking it away?

KROGSTAD. Don't pretend you don't know. It's obvious that
your friend doesn't want to bump into me again – and it's
also obvious who I've got to thank for getting me the sack.

NORA. But –

KROGSTAD. Never mind. I'm telling you: use your
influence to see it doesn't happen.

NORA. Mr Krogstad, I don't have any influence.

KROGSTAD. That's not what you said just now.

NORA. I didn't mean . . . you shouldn't have . . . What
makes you think I can influence my husband?

KROGSTAD. I've known your husband for years. He can be
influenced, Mr Manager, just like anyone else.

NORA. If you're impertinent about my husband, you can
leave my house.

KROGSTAD. Oh, very brave.

NORA. I'm not afraid of you. Not any more. As soon as it's
New Year, I'll be finished with the whole business.

KROGSTAD (*with control*). Mrs Helmer, understand one
thing: if it comes to it, I'll fight for my job as if I was
fighting for my life.

NORA. That's obvious.

KROGSTAD. The money's not important. It's something
else. It's . . . ah . . . You must be aware that some time ago,
a long time ago, I . . . slipped up a little.

NORA. I heard.

KROGSTAD. It never came to court. But it . . . blocked me,
barred doors against me. That's why I began my business.
You know what I mean. I had to make a living – and I
wasn't one of the worst. But now I want done with it. My
sons are growing up; for their sakes I want to be
respectable again, as much as possible. That job at the
Bank was the first step – and now your husband is kicking
me down to the mud again.

NORA. Mr Krogstad, for heaven's sake, I can't help you.

KROGSTAD. Can't? Won't. But I think you must.

NORA. You'd tell my husband I owe you money?

KROGSTAD. Why not?

NORA. How can you? (*fighting back tears.*) My secret, my pride, my treasure – and he hears it from *you*. It's horrid. It'll be so *awkward*.

KROGSTAD. *Awkward?*

NORA (*angrily*). Do it, do it, and see where it gets you. My husband'll see what sort of man you are. You'll never get your job back.

KROGSTAD. What I meant was, is it just awkwardness you're afraid of?

NORA. As soon as my husband hears, he'll pay you every penny. Naturally. At once. And then we'll be rid of you for good.

KROGSTAD (*closer*). Mrs Helmer. Pay attention. Either you've a very bad memory, or you know nothing of business. I'd better remind you.

NORA. What?

KROGSTAD. Your husband was ill. You came to me for a loan. Four thousand, eight hundred kroner.

NORA. Where else was I to turn?

KROGSTAD. I said I'd find the money –

NORA. You did find it.

KROGSTAD. – on certain conditions. You were so upset about your husband, so eager for the money to cure him, I don't think you noticed the conditions. So I'd better remind you. I said I'd find the money; I wrote a contract.

NORA. And I signed it.

KROGSTAD. That's right. But underneath your signature was a clause saying that your father would guarantee the repayments. Your father should have signed that clause.

NORA. He did.

KROGSTAD. I left the date blank. Your father was to fill it in: the date he signed the document. You remember that, Mrs Helmer?

NORA. I think so.

KROGSTAD. I gave you the contract, to post to your father. You remember that?

NORA. Yes.

KROGSTAD. You must have done it immediately, because you brought it back in less than a week, with your father's signature. Then I gave you the money.

NORA. And I've been paying it back, haven't I? As arranged?

KROGSTAD. Let's keep to the point, Mrs Helmer. That must have been a very difficult time for you.

NORA. Yes.

KROGSTAD. Your father was desperately ill.

NORA. Yes.

KROGSTAD. In fact he died soon after?

NORA. Yes.

KROGSTAD. Mrs Helmer, can you remember the exact date? The date he died?

NORA. 29th September.

KROGSTAD. Yes indeed. I checked. That's what makes it so extraordinary . . .

He takes out a paper.

So hard to explain . . .

NORA. What's hard to explain?

KROGSTAD. The fact that your father signed this document three days after he died.

NORA. What d'you mean?

KROGSTAD. Your father died on the 29th September. But he dated his signature – here, look – on the 2nd October. As I say, Mrs Helmer: extraordinary.

NORA says nothing.

Can *you* explain it?

No answer.

Even more extraordinary: the words 2nd October, and the year, aren't in your father's writing, but in someone else's. I think I know whose. It's easily explained. Your father forgot to date his signature, so someone else dated it, someone who didn't know the date he died. But none of that's important. What's important is that the signature's genuine. There's no doubt about that, is there, Mrs Helmer? This is your father's signature?

Short pause. Then NORA *lifts her head and looks defiantly at him.*

NORA. No, it isn't. I signed father's name.

KROGSTAD. Mrs Helmer, you shouldn't have admitted that.

NORA. You'll get your money.

KROGSTAD. Tell me: why didn't you send your father the contract?

NORA. He was too ill. I couldn't. I'd have had to tell him what the money was for. He was so ill, I couldn't tell him my husband was at death's door too. I couldn't.

KROGSTAD. You should have cancelled the trip abroad.

NORA. My husband's life! How could I?

KROGSTAD. It never worried you, that you were cheating me?

NORA. I couldn't let it. I couldn't consider you. I hated you . . . all that coldness, those conditions, when you knew how ill my husband was.

KROGSTAD. Mrs Helmer, you've obviously no idea just what you've done. But I'll tell you, it was nothing more or less than my own . . . mistake. All those years ago.

NORA. You took a risk, that kind of risk, to save your wife?

KROGSTAD. The law's not interested in reasons.

NORA. Then it's a fool.

KROGSTAD. Fool or not, it's what you'll be judged by, if I take this document to court.

NORA. Nonsense. A daughter can't save her dying father   ˙
from care and worry? A wife can't help her sick husband?
I know nothing about the law, but there must be laws

about that. You were supposed to be a lawyer – didn't you know about them? You can't have been much of a lawyer.

KROGSTAD. Maybe not. But contracts, the kind of contract you made with me, I know all about those. You understand? Good. Do as you please, but remember one thing: if I lose everything a second time, you keep me company.

He bows and goes out through the hall. NORA *is lost in thought for a moment, then tosses her head.*

NORA. Ridiculous. He was trying to scare me. I'm not so silly.

She starts gathering the CHILDREN's *clothes. Stops suddenly.*

But suppose – ? No. I did it for love.

CHILDREN (*at the door, left*). Mummy, he's gone, the man.

NORA. That's right, he's gone. Don't tell anyone he came. Not even Daddy.

CHILDREN. Mummy, let's play another game.

NORA. No. No. Not now.

CHILDREN. You promised.

NORA. I can't just now. I'm too busy. Go in. Darlings, go in.

She manages to get them out of the room and shuts the door. She sits on the sofa, takes up some sewing and does a stitch or two, then stops.

No!

She puts the sewing down, goes to the hall door and calls.

Helene! Bring in the Christmas tree.

She goes to table, left, opens a drawer then stops again.

I can't. I can't.

The MAID *brings in the tree.*

MAID. Where shall I put it, madam?

NORA. There, in the middle.

MAID. Can I get anything else?

NORA. No thankyou. I've all I need.

The MAID *puts the tree down, and goes.* NORA *starts trimming it.*

NORA. A candle here . . . flowers here . . . That dreadful man. No, no, it's all right. The tree, the tree must be beautiful. Torvald, I'll do whatever you want. I'll sing for you, dance for you –

HELMER *comes in, with papers.*

Ah! Back so soon?

HELMER. That's right. Has anyone called?

NORA. No.

HELMER. I saw Krogstad at the gate.

NORA. Krogstad? Ah. He was here, just for a moment.

HELMER. Nora, I know what it is. He was asking you to put in a word for him.

NORA. Yes.

HELMER. You were to pretend it was your idea? You were to pretend he hadn't been here? Did he ask that too?

NORA. Oh, Torvald –

HELMER. Nora, how could you? Talk to a man like that, make promises, lie to me?

NORA. Lie?

HELMER. No one called, you said. (*wagging his finger.*) Little bird must never do that again. Little bird must only sing pretty songs. No nasties. (*putting his arm round her waist.*) Isn't that right? Of course it is. (*letting her go.*) Let's have no more about it. (*sitting by the stove.*) It's lovely and warm in here.

He turns over his papers. NORA *busies herself with the tree for a moment, then:*

NORA. Torvald . . .

HELMER. What?

NORA. I can't wait for Boxing Day. The Stenborgs. The fancy-dress party.

HELMER. And I can't wait to see your surprise.

NORA. I'm such a goose.

HELMER. What d'you mean?

NORA. The surprise. I can't think what to wear. Every idea I have seems silly, silly.

HELMER. Dear little Nora realises that at last?

NORA (*behind him, arms on the back of his chair*). Torvald, are you busy?

HELMER. Mm?

NORA. Those papers.

TORVALD. Bank business.

NORA. Already?

HELMER. The retiring manager has authorised me to review staffing and duties. I have to do it this week, have it ready by New Year.

NORA. That's why poor Mr Krogstad –

HELMER. Hm.

NORA (*leaning over the chair, playing with his hair at the neck*). Torvald, if you hadn't been so busy, I was going to ask you a big favour.

HELMER. What favour?

NORA. No one has taste like yours. I want to look nice for the fancy-dress party. Torvald, won't you settle it? Tell me what to wear, what I ought to go as?

HELMER. Aha! My independent little creature needs a helping hand?

NORA. I can't manage without you.

HELMER. I'll think about it. We'll sort it out.

NORA. You are nice.

She goes to the tree. Pause.

Aren't these red flowers pretty? Did Krogstad do something really terrible?

HELMER. Forged someone's name. Can you imagine?

NORA. If he'd no alternative – ?

HELMER. If he'd made a mistake . . . I'm not heartless; I wouldn't condemn a man for one mistake.

NORA. Torvald . . .

HELMER. Plenty of people make mistakes, admit them, take the punishment –

NORA. Punishment?

HELMER. But not Krogstad. He wriggled out of it. That's what I can't forgive.

NORA. You can't?

HELMER. Imagine someone like that. Lies, hypocrisy, tricking everyone in sight, his family, his wife, his children. That's the worst thing of all, the children.

NORA. What d'you mean?

HELMER. An atmosphere like that, a stench of lies and deceit, poisons the whole household. Each breath children take in a house like that is a lungful of deadly germs.

NORA (*going closer*). D'you really believe that?

HELMER. Darling, when I worked in the law I saw hardly anything else. Almost always, when people go bad young in life, the cause is a deceitful mother.

NORA. Just – a mother?

HELMER. It's usually the mother. Though a father can be just as bad. Every lawyer knows. This Krogstad has been poisoning his children for years. Lies, cheating . . . you see what·I mean, depraved.

He holds out his hands to her.

That's why darling little Nora must promise: never ask me to help him. Mm? Mm? Take hold. What's the matter?

Take hold. There. I just couldn't work with him. People like that literally make me ill.

NORA *lets go his hands and crosses to the other side of the tree.*

NORA. It's so hot in here. And I've such a lot to do.

HELMER (*getting up, bundling up his papers*). I must try to get through some of this before dinner. And there's your fancy dress to think about. And I may – I *may* – have a little something in gold paper, to hang on the tree. (*putting his hand on her head.*) My darling, my little songbird.

He goes into the study and shuts the door. Pause. Then NORA *whispers:*

NORA. It can't be. No. It *can't.*

ANNE-MARIE *appears at the door, left.*

ANNE-MARIE. The children are crying for you. Shall I bring them in?

NORA. No! No! I don't want to see them. Stay with them.

ANNE-MARIE. As madam wishes.

She closes the door.

NORA (*white with terror*). Poison them? My children, my family?

Pause. Then she lifts her head.

Never. Impossible.

Curtain.

Act Two

The same. In the corner beside the piano, the Christmas tree stands stripped of its decorations and with its candles burned to stumps. On the sofa, NORA's evening cape. NORA, alone in the room, is pacing restlessly. She picks up her cape, then puts it down again.

NORA. Someone's coming.

She goes to the door and listens.

No one. Of course not, it's Christmas Day. Not tomorrow, either. Unless –

She opens the door and looks out.

No. No letters. The box is empty. (*Pacing.*) Stupid. Of course he didn't mean it. Things like that don't happen. They don't. I've got three small children.

ANNE-MARIE comes from the room left, with a large cardboard box.

ANNE-MARIE. I've found it. The box with the fancy dress.

NORA. Thanks. Put it on the table.

ANNE-MARIE (*as she does so*). It needs mending.

NORA. I wish I'd torn it to pieces.

ANNE-MARIE. You can fix it. Just a little patience.

NORA. I'll ask Mrs Linde to help.

ANNE-MARIE. Out again? In this weather? You'll catch a chill, make yourself poorly.

NORA. Never mind that . . . Are the children all right?

ANNE-MARIE. Playing with their Christmas presents. If only –

NORA. Are they still asking for me?

ANNE-MARIE. They're used to having their Mummy there.

NORA. No, Anne-Marie. I've no time any more.

ANNE-MARIE. Well, little ones get used to anything.

NORA. D'you think so? D'you think if their Mummy went far away, they'd forget her?

ANNE-MARIE. Far away!

NORA. Anne-Marie, I want to ask you something. I've often wondered. How could you do it? How could you bear it? To give your own child to be fostered.

ANNE-MARIE. I'd no choice. How else could I have been nurse to baby Nora?

NORA. But did you *want* to?

ANNE-MARIE. To get such a good position? A poor girl in trouble. *He* wasn't about to help.

NORA. I suppose your daughter's long forgotten you.

ANNE-MARIE. No, no. She wrote to me, when she was confirmed, and when she got married.

NORA (*hugging her*). Dear old Anne-Marie. You were such a good mother to me when I was little.

ANNE-MARIE. Poor baby, you'd no one else.

NORA. I know if my little ones had no one else, you'd . . .
Tsk, tsk. (*opening the box.*) Go back to them. I must . . .
Tomorrow you'll see how pretty I'll look.

ANNE-MARIE. You'll be the prettiest one there.

She goes into the room left. NORA *starts taking things out of the
box, then pushes it aside.*

NORA. If I dared go out. If I knew no one would come,
nothing would happen. Stupid. No one's coming. Don't
think about it. Brush my muff. What pretty gloves. Think
about something else. One, two, three, four, five six . . .
(*screams.*) Ah! Someone's there!

She tries to go to the door, but can't move. MRS LINDE *comes in
from the hall, where she has taken off her coat.*

It's you, Kristine. There's no one else out there? Oh,
thanks for coming.

MRS LINDE. They said you'd called and asked for me.

NORA. I was passing. Something you can perhaps help me
with. Let's sit on the sofa. Look. There's a fancy-dress party
tomorrow. The Stenborgs. The apartment upstairs.
Torvald wants me to go as a Neapolitan fishergirl, and
dance the tarantella I learned in Capri.

MRS LINDE. Quite a show.

NORA. Torvald insists. This is the dress. Torvald had it made
for me. But it's all torn . . . I don't . . .

MRS LINDE. It's easy. The frill's come undone, here and
here. That's all. Have you a needle and thread? Ah yes.

NORA. It's kind of you.

MRS LINDE (*sewing*). So tomorrow you'll be all dressed up? I'll pop in, see how you look. I never said thankyou for that lovely evening, yesterday.

NORA (*getting up, pacing*). It could have been even better. If you'd come to town sooner. Well. Torvald certainly knows how to make a place welcoming.

MRS LINDE. And so do you. Not your father's daughter for nothing. Is Dr Rank always as gloomy as yesterday?

NORA. He was bad. He's seriously ill. Lesions in the spine. Poor man. His father was horrible. Woman after woman. That's why the son . . . tainted blood . . .

MRS LINDE (*putting down the sewing*). Nora, how do you *know* about things like that?

NORA (*pacing*). Oh, fiddle, if you've got three children, people are always calling. Married women. Medical things..they mention this and that . . . they know.

MRS LINDE (*resuming her sewing, after a short pause*). Does he come every day, Dr Rank?

NORA. He's been Torvald's best friend for years. Since they were children. My friend too. One of the family.

MRS LINDE. You're sure he's . . . all he seems? Not just . . . making himself agreeable?

NORA. Of course not. Why d'you think so?

MRS LINDE. When you introduced us yesterday, he said he'd often heard my name here. But your husband had no idea who I was. So how could Dr Rank – ?

NORA. That's no mystery. Torvald's so fond of me, wants me all to himself, he says. He was always so jealous, if I mentioned people I'd known before. So I didn't. But I often gossip with Dr Rank. He enjoys all that.

MRS LINDE. Nora, you are a child, sometimes. Listen to me. I'm older, more experienced. Finish all this with Dr Rank.

NORA. Finish all what?

MRS LINDE. Yesterday you talked about a rich admirer, someone who'd leave you all his money –

NORA. That's right. Imaginary, alas. What of it?

MRS LINDE. Is Dr Rank . . . well off?

NORA. Oh yes.

MRS LINDE. No dependants?

NORA. What about it?

MRS LINDE. Calls here every day?

NORA. I told you.

MRS LINDE. How could a good friend be so . . . presumptuous?

NORA. I don't know what you mean.

MRS LINDE. Nora. Don't pretend. D'you think I can't guess who lent you all that money?

NORA. You're crazy. A friend, who calls in every day – d'you think I could bear it?

MRS LINDE. It isn't him?

NORA. Of course it isn't him. I'd never have dreamed . . . In any case, in those days he hadn't a penny to lend. He came into money later.

MRS LINDE. That could be lucky for you.

NORA. Dr Rank? You don't think I'd ever ask him . . . ? Though I'm sure if I did . . .

MRS LINDE. Which you won't.

NORA. Of course I won't. But if I *did* . . .

MRS LINDE. Behind your husband's back?

NORA. I'll finish with the other one. That's also behind his back. I've got to finish it.

MRS LINDE. I said so yesterday. But –

NORA (*pacing*). It's easy for a man to end that kind of thing. But a wife . . .

MRS LINDE. Her husband could do it.

NORA. Oh no. (*stands still.*) When you pay off a debt, you do get your contract back?

MRS LINDE. I imagine so.

NORA. And you can tear it to bits, burn the nasty, filthy thing.

MRS LINDE *looks at her, then puts down the sewing and goes to her.*

MRS LINDE. What is it, Nora?

NORA. What?

MRS LINDE. Something's happened since yesterday.

NORA (*going close*). Kristine . . . (*listens.*) Sh! Torvald. Look, go in there, with the children, d'you mind? Torvald hates seeing dress-making. Anne-Marie'll help you.

MRS LINDE gathers some of her things.

MRS LINDE. All right, but I won't leave the house till we've talked about this properly.

She goes into the room, left, as HELMER comes in from the hall.

NORA (*going to greet him*). Darling. I've been waiting . . .

HELMER. Was that the dressmaker?

NORA. No, Kristine. She's helping me. I'll look splendid.

HELMER. Wasn't it a good idea?

NORA. And aren't I good to do it?

HELMER (*chucking her under the chin*). Good, to agree with your husband? Tut, tut, tut. Well, I'll keep out of the way. You'll be wanting to try it on.

NORA. You've work to do?

HELMER. Yes. (*showing her a sheaf of papers.*) I've just been into the Bank . . .

He is about to go into the study, when she stops him.

NORA. Torvald.

HELMER. Yes?

NORA. If your little squirrel asked for something, very, very nicely . . .

HELMER. Yes . . . ?

NORA. Would you do it?

HELMER. Depends what it was.

NORA. If you'd be good and kind and say yes, little squirrel would dance and do lots of tricks.

HELMER. Come on.

NORA. Little songbird would chirp and sing in every room.

HELMER. Songbird does that anyway.

NORA. I'd play fairies, dance in the moonlight. Torvald.

HELMER. Nora: this isn't what you were asking this morning?

NORA (*going to him*). Eth, Torvald. I'th athking vewwy nithely.

HELMER. How can you bring that up again?

NORA. Please. For me. Give Krogstad his job back. Please.

HELMER. Nora, darling, I've given Mrs Linde Krogstad's job.

NORA. And that was very kind of you. But surely you can sack some other clerk instead of Krogstad.

HELMER. I don't believe this. Obstinacy! Because *you* made him a stupid promise, *I'm* supposed to –

NORA. Torvald, that isn't why. It's for your sake. He writes articles in dreadful newspapers. You told me so. He can do you a lot of harm. I'm scared of him, scared –

HELMER. Because of the past.

NORA. What d'you mean?

HELMER. Well, obviously: your father.

NORA. Oh. Yes. When those spiteful men wrote about him in the papers. Lies and slander. He'd have lost his job if you hadn't been sent to enquire, if you hadn't been so kind to him, so helpful . . .

HELMER. Nora, there's a vital difference between your father and me. Your father wasn't a respected public official. I am. And I hope I'll always be so, as long as I stay in office.

NORA. Who knows what terrible things they'll do, those men? We could be so happy here, Torvald, you, me, the children, in our carefree, peaceful home. All I ask, please –

HELMER. It's because you plead for him that I can't help him. Everyone at the Bank knows I've sacked him. If it comes out that the new manager changes his mind when his wife demands it –

NORA. What's wrong with that?

HELMER. You mean if my little terrier got her way? I'd be a laughing stock. Before the whole staff. They'd think anyone could work on me. I couldn't have that. In any case, I can't take Krogstad back, under any circumstances.

NORA. Why not?

HELMER. I could overlook his character if I had to –

NORA. Of course you could.

HELMER. And they say he's a good worker. But I knew him when we were both children. We were friends – one of those stupid friendships you regret later in life. I mean, we used first names. And that tactless oaf won't let it lie, even now, even when we're in company. Thinks it's quite in order to stroll up any time he feels like it – 'Hey, Torvald, Torvald . . . ' Highly embarrassing. It would make my position in the Bank impossible.

NORA. Torvald, you're joking.

HELMER. You think so?

NORA. I can't believe you're so small-minded.

HELMER. You think I'm small-minded?

NORA. Of course I don't. So –

HELMER. Right. You think I'm small-minded. Small-minded. I'll settle this right away.

He goes to the hall door and calls:

Helene!

NORA. What are you doing?

HELMER (*fishing among his papers*). Settling it.

The MAID *comes in.*

Here. Take this letter. Run downstairs, find a porter and tell him to deliver it. Right now. The address is on it. Here's some money.

MAID. Yes, sir.

She goes. HELMER *gathers his papers.*

Now then, little Miss Stubborn . . .

NORA (*hardly able to breathe*). Torvald, what was it, that letter?

HELMER. Krogstad's dismissal.

NORA. Call her back, Torvald. There's still time. Oh

Torvald, call her back – for me, for you, for the children. Please, Torvald, please. You don't know what it'll do to us.

HELMER. Too late.

NORA. Yes, too late.

HELMER. Darling, I don't blame you for being upset, even though it's so insulting to me. That's right, insulting. To think that I'd be afraid of that . . . that worn-out pen-pusher. I don't blame you, because it shows how much you love me. (*taking her in his arms*.) My own dear darling, this is how it'll be. Whatever happens, I'll be strong enough, brave enough. I'm a man, I'll carry the burden alone.

NORA (*terrified*). You mean – ?

HELMER. All of it.

NORA (*recovering her composure*). You'll never have to do that.

HELMER. Darling, we'll share it, then: husband and wife. That's how it'll be. (*stroking her*.) Happy? It's all right, all right. Poor little trembling dove. Silly, silly. Why don't you play that tarantella? Practise your tambourine. I'll go into the office and shut the door. I won't hear; make all the noise you want.

He goes to the door, then turns.

When Rank comes, tell him where to find me.

He nods to her, goes into the study with his papers and shuts the door.

NORA *stands rooted, terrified and unsure.*

NORA (*whisper*). He was ready to do it. He can. He will. Nothing can stop him. No. He mustn't. But how? What?

Doorbell, off.

Rank! Anything . . .

She passes her hands over her face, pulls herself together and goes to open the door to the hall. RANK is in the hall, hanging up his coat. During the scene which follows, it begins to get dark.

Hello, Doctor. I recognised your ring. Don't disturb Torvald: he's busy just now.

RANK. What about you?

He comes into the room, and she shuts the door.

NORA. You know I've always got time for you.

RANK. Thankyou. I'll make the most of it, as long as I can.

NORA. As long as you can?

RANK. What's the matter?

NORA. It sounded odd, that's all. As if you were expecting something to happen.

RANK. I've been expecting it for a long time. Not quite so soon, that's all.

NORA (*taking his arm*). What is it? Doctor, tell me.

RANK (*sitting by the stove*). I'm done for. Incurable.

NORA (*sighing with relief*). Oh, it's you.

RANK. No point lying to oneself. Mrs Helmer, I'm in the worst state of all my patients. I've spent the last few days reviewing my own case. Terminal. In a month I'll be rotting in the churchyard.

NORA. Don't be horrid.

RANK. It is horrid. And it won't get any less horrid. One more examination; as soon as that's done, I'll know the exact moment when the decline begins. Mrs Helmer, one thing. Torvald's a fastidious man. Ugliness disgusts him. I won't have him in my sickroom.

NORA. Doctor –

RANK. Absolutely not. Door barred. As soon as I know the worst, I'll send you one of my cards, marked with a cross. You'll know that the dissolution, the vileness, has begun.

NORA. You're being ridiculous. I wanted you to be in such a good mood . . .

RANK. With Death at my elbow? For someone else's guilt? How fair is that? I think it's the same in every family in the world: retribution, one kind or another, unavoidable –

NORA (*covering her ears*). La, la, la! Be nice, be nice.

RANK. It's a joke. The whole thing's a joke. My father indulged himself; my poor blameless spine has to pay the bill.

NORA (*at the table, left*). Foie gras? Asparagus?

RANK. And truffles.

NORA. Oysters.

RANK. Naturally.

NORA. Port, champagne – what a shame such delicious things take it out on our poor old bones.

RANK. Especially poor old bones that never had the pleasure of them.

NORA. That's the worst of all.

RANK (*looking hard at her*). H'm.

NORA (*after a short pause*). Why did you smile?

RANK. You were laughing.

NORA. Doctor, you smiled.

RANK (*getting up*). You're even wilder than I thought.

NORA. I'm in a wild mood today.

RANK. So it seems.

NORA (*both hands on his shoulders*). Doctor, darling, please don't die. For Torvald, for me, don't die.

RANK. You'll get over me. Out of sight, out of mind.

NORA (*distressed*). Don't say that.

RANK. You'll find someone else. People do.

NORA. Who does? Who will?

RANK. You. Torvald. You've started already. Mrs Linde – why else was she here yesterday?

NORA. Hoho. You're jealous.

RANK. Of course I am. She'll take my place. When I'm dead and done for, she'll be the one –

NORA. Sh! She's in there.

RANK. You see?

NORA. She's doing some sewing. What a bear you are! (*sitting on the sofa.*) Be good now, Doctor, and tomorrow you'll see

how nicely I dance. You can pretend it's all for you – well,
for Torvald too.

She starts taking things out of the box.

Doctor Rank, sit down here. I want to show you
something.

RANK (*sitting*). What?

NORA. These.

RANK. Silk stockings.

NORA. Aren't they pretty? It's dark now, but tomorrow . . .
No no, look at the feet. Oh well, the legs as well.

RANK. Hm –

NORA. What's the matter? Don't you think they'll fit?

RANK. I've no possible way of telling.

NORA (*glancing at him*). Tut tut!

She flicks his ear with the stockings.

Bad boy!

RANK. What other delights am I to see?

NORA. None at all, you're far too naughty.

Humming, she turns the things over. Short pause.

RANK. When I sit here with you, so friendly, I can't . . . it's
hard to . . . what would my life have been like if I'd never
known this house?

NORA (*smiling*). You really feel at home here.

RANK (*low, looking straight ahead*). To have to leave it forever –

NORA. Fiddlededee. You don't.

RANK (*as before*). To have to leave without a single token of
    what it's meant to me . . . hardly a backward glance . . .
    just an empty place for the next person, anyone, to fill . . .

NORA. What if I asked you . . . No!

RANK. Asked what?

NORA. For a token. Of friendship . . .

RANK. Go on.

NORA. I mean, a really big favour.

RANK. I'd be delighted –

NORA. You don't know what it is, yet.

RANK. Tell me.

NORA. I can't. It's too much. Advice, help, a favour –

RANK. The bigger the better. I can't imagine what you
    mean. Tell me. Don't you trust me?

NORA. You're my truest, dearest friend. You know you are.
    Doctor, it's something you can help me prevent. You know
    how Torvald loves me . . . deeply, beyond words . . . he'd
    give his life . . .

RANK (*leaning forward to her*). Nora. D'you think he's the only
    one?

NORA (*starting*). What?

RANK. The only one who'd give his life for you?

NORA (*heavily*). Ah.

RANK. I swore I'd tell you before I . . . went. Now. Nora, now you know. And you know that you can rely on me, as on no one else.

NORA (*getting up, calmly and evenly*). Excuse me.

RANK (*sitting still, but making room for her to pass*). Nora –

NORA (*at the hall door*). Helene, bring the lamps.

She crosses to the stove.

Doctor, dear Doctor, that was uncalled for.

RANK (*getting up*). To love you as much as . . . another man? Uncalled for?

NORA. To tell me. There was no need.

RANK. You knew?

The MAID *brings in the lamps, puts them on the table and goes out again.*

Nora . . . Mrs Helmer . . . are you saying you knew?

NORA. I don't know what I knew. How could you be so . . . clumsy?

RANK. All that matters is, you know I'm at your service, body and soul. Tell me what it is.

NORA (*staring at him*). What?

RANK. Please.

NORA. Not now.

RANK. Don't punish me. Let me help you . . . whatever a man can do.

NORA. There's nothing you can do. I don't really need help. It was just . . . a game, a silly game.

She sits on the rocking chair, and smiles at him.

Doctor, what a man you are! Aren't you embarrassed, now, in proper light?

RANK. Not in the least. But perhaps I'd better go . . . forever.

NORA. Of course not. Come. Don't change. You know what it means to Torvald.

RANK. And to you?

NORA. I'm always delighted to see you.

RANK. That's why I . . . I don't understand you. I've often thought that you enjoy my company almost as much as Torvald's.

NORA. Company. We enjoy some people's company. Others, we love.

RANK. Yes.

NORA. When I was a child, I loved Daddy more than anyone. But I kept thinking how nice it would be to slip down to the servants' room. They never told me what to do. They were such fun to talk to.

RANK. And it's *their* place I've taken.

NORA *jumps up and goes to him.*

NORA. I didn't mean that. I didn't mean that. It's just that . . . Torvald and Daddy . . . Don't you see?

The MAID *comes in.*

MAID. Madam . . .

She whispers to her and gives her a visiting card.

NORA (*glancing at it*). Ah!

She puts it in her pocket.

RANK. Nothing wrong?

NORA. No, no. Just . . . my new dress.

RANK. It's in there, your dress.

NORA. One of them is. This is another one. I ordered it . . . I don't want Torvald to know.

RANK. Hoho. *That* was the great big secret.

NORA. Yes. Go in to him now. He's in the study. Keep him there.

RANK. Don't worry. He won't get away.

He goes into the study.

NORA (*to the* MAID). He's in the kitchen? Waiting?

MAID. He came to the back door.

NORA. You told him no one was in?

MAID. It didn't do any good.

NORA. He wouldn't go?

MAID. He said he had to talk to you.

NORA. Well, bring him in. But quietly. Helene, keep it a secret. It's a surprise for my husband.

MAID. Yes, madam. I understand.

She goes.

NORA. It's happening. I can't stop it. I can't. I can't.

She locks the study door. The MAID *ushers* KROGSTAD *in from the hall, and shuts the door behind him. He is wearing boots and a fur coat and cap.* NORA *hurries to him.*

NORA. Keep your voice down. My husband's here.

KROGSTAD. Doesn't matter.

NORA. What d'you want?

KROGSTAD. I want you to explain something.

NORA. Be quick.

KROGSTAD. You know I've been sacked?

NORA. There was nothing I could do. I tried, but it was no good.

KROGSTAD. Your husband cares so little for you? He knows the harm I can do you, and still he –

NORA. What makes you think he knows?

KROGSTAD. Ah. I thought he didn't. I could hardly imagine Torvald Helmer being so brave –

NORA. I'll thank you to show a little more respect.

KROGSTAD. As much as he deserves. But since milady's kept the whole thing so carefully to herself, I imagine it's sunk in since yesterday, exactly what you've done.

NORA. No thanks to you.

KROGSTAD. I'm a very bad lawyer, remember?

NORA. What is it you want?

KROGSTAD. Mrs Helmer, I was anxious about you. I've had you in my thoughts all day. A cashier, a pen-pusher, a nonentity like me, can still feel sympathy.

NORA. Feel some, then. For my children.

KROGSTAD. As much as you and your husband felt for me? Never mind. I just want to tell you, there's no need to take this business to heart. There'll be no accusations made from this side.

NORA. I didn't think there would be.

KROGSTAD. It can be settled easily. Amicably. No one has to know but the three of us.

NORA. My husband must never find out.

KROGSTAD. How will you prevent that? Are you saying you can pay the balance?

NORA. Not at the moment.

KROGSTAD. You've some quick way to find it?

NORA. None I intend to use.

KROGSTAD. In any case, it wouldn't help now. However much you pay, I'm not giving up that paper.

NORA. What are you going to do with it?

KROGSTAD. Keep it, that's all. Safe. No third party need ever hear of it. So if you'd any crazy ideas –

NORA. I had.

KROGSTAD. – of running away, for example –

NORA. Who told you?

KROGSTAD. – don't bother.

NORA. How did you know I – ?

KROGSTAD. We all think of that at first. I did, too. But I
    wasn't brave enough.

NORA (*tonelessly*). Neither am I.

KROGSTAD (*lightly*). Exactly. You aren't brave enough,
    either.

NORA. No.

KROGSTAD. It would be stupid, anyway. Once the first
    storm at home blows over . . . I've a letter here for your
    husband.

NORA. Telling him everything?

KROGSTAD. As objectively as possible.

NORA (*blurted*). He mustn't see it. Tear it up. I'll find the
    money.

KROGSTAD. I'm sorry, Mrs Helmer, but I thought I just
    told you –

NORA. I don't mean the loan. Tell me how much you're
    demanding from my husband, and I'll find the money.

KROGSTAD. I'm not asking him for money.

NORA. What, then?

KROGSTAD. I told you. Mrs Helmer, I want to make myself
    respectable. I want to get on. I want your husband to help
    me. I've had clean hands for eighteen months, and things

have been very difficult. I didn't mind: I was working my way up, step by step. But now I've been sacked, I won't be satisfied with simply getting my job back. I want something better. Reinstatement – in a higher position. Your husband will find one –

NORA. He won't.

KROGSTAD. I know him. He won't dare argue. Once I'm back, just wait and see! In one year – less – I'll be the Manager's right hand. Not Torvald Helmer, but Nils Krogstad, will run that bank.

NORA. No. Never.

KROGSTAD. You mean you'll – ?

NORA. I'm brave enough now.

KROGSTAD. You don't scare me. A fine lady, airs and graces –

NORA. Wait and see.

KROGSTAD. Under the ice, perhaps? In the deep, dark depths? Floating up in the spring, bloated, unrecognisable, your hair fallen out –

NORA. You don't scare me.

KROGSTAD. And you don't scare me. Mrs Helmer, no one does things like that. In any case, what good would it do? I'd still have him just where I wanted him.

NORA. You mean even after I . . . even if I was – ?

KROGSTAD. Have you forgotten? I own your reputation.

NORA *stares at him speechlessly.*

So, you stand warned. Don't do anything stupid. Helmer
will get my letter. I'll wait for a reply. And remember this:
it was him, your husband, who forced me to do this. I'll
never forgive him for that. Good afternoon.

*He goes out through the hall. NORA, at the door, holds it open and
listens.*

NORA. He's going. He's not leaving the letter. Of course he
is. (*opening the door further.*) What is it? He's standing there.
Not going downstairs. He's changing his mind. He's –

*A letter falls into the box, and we hear KROGSTAD's steps dying
away as he goes down the stairs. With a stifled shriek, NORA
crosses to the table by the sofa. Short pause.*

In the letter-box.

She creeps across to the hall door.

Torvald, oh Torvald, he's finished us.

MRS LINDE *comes in from the room left. She carries the fancy
dress.*

MRS LINDE. That didn't take long. Shall we try it on – ?

NORA (*hoarse whisper*). Kristine, come here.

MRS LINDE (*throwing the costume down on the sofa*). What's the
matter? You look terrified.

NORA. Come here. D'you see that letter?

MRS LINDE. Yes.

NORA. It's from Krogstad.

MRS LINDE. The man who lent you the money?

NORA. Now Torvald'll know everything.

MRS LINDE. It's really best, for both of you.

NORA. You don't understand. I forged a signature.

MRS LINDE. For heaven's sake!

NORA. Kristine, you must speak for me.

MRS LINDE. What d'you mean?

NORA. If I . . . go crazy.

MRS LINDE. Nora.

NORA. Or if anything happened . . . if I had to go away . . .

MRS LINDE. What are you saying, Nora?

NORA. If someone else wants to take all the blame – d'you
understand? –

MRS LINDE. Yes.

NORA. *Then* you must speak for me. I'm not crazy. I know
what I'm doing. And I'm telling you: no one else knew
anything about it. I did it, not another soul. Remember.

MRS LINDE. I still don't understand.

NORA. Why should you understand? What's going to
happen . . . is a miracle!

MRS LINDE. A miracle?

NORA. It's a miracle. And it mustn't happen, Kristine,
mustn't happen for all the world.

MRS LINDE. I'm going to see Krogstad.

NORA. No. He'll hurt you.

MRS LINDE. Once, he'd have done anything for my sake.

NORA. Krogstad?

MRS LINDE. Where does he live?

NORA. I don't . . . (*fishing in her pocket.*) Yes, here's his card. But the letter, the letter . . .

HELMER (*in his room, knocking*). Nora!

NORA (*scream*). Ah! What is it?

HELMER. Don't be alarmed. We won't come in. You've locked the door. Are you trying the dress?

NORA. Yes. Yes. I'll be so pretty, Torvald.

MRS LINDE (*who has read the card*). It's just round the corner.

NORA. It's too late. We're finished. The letter's in the box. There, in the hall.

MRS LINDE. And your husband has the key?

NORA. The only one.

MRS LINDE. Krogstad must ask for his letter back, unopened. He must find some excuse . . .

NORA. But it's now that Torvald always –

MRS LINDE. Delay him. Go in there. I'll be as quick as I can.

She hurries out through the hall. NORA *goes to* HELMER*'s door, opens it and peeps in.*

HELMER (*out of sight*). Ah! We can use our own front room again. Come on, Rank, now we'll see – (*in the doorway.*) What's the matter?

NORA. What d'you mean, darling?

HELMER. Rank said I was to expect a transformation.

RANK (*in the doorway*). I must have been mistaken.

NORA. No one's to admire my dress till tomorrow morning.

HELMER. Nora, you look worn out. Have you been
practising too hard?

NORA. I haven't been practising.

HELMER. You ought to.

NORA. I will, Torvald. But you've got to help. I can't
remember it all.

HELMER. We'll soon bring it back.

NORA. Yes, Torvald, help me. Promise. I'm terrified . . . all
those people. Help me, this evening. No business. No pen,
no papers. Please, Torvald.

HELMER. I promise. This evening I'm yours, and yours
alone. Little Miss Helpless. Just a moment, though –

He makes for the hall door.

NORA. Where are you going?

HELMER. Just to see if the post has come.

NORA. Torvald, don't.

HELMER. What's the matter?

NORA. Torvald, I beg you. There isn't any.

HELMER. I'll just have a look.

He is about to go, when NORA *runs to the piano and plays the first few bars of the tarantella. He stops.*

Aha!

NORA. I can't dance tomorrow, unless I rehearse with you.

HELMER (*going to her*). You're really nervous?

NORA. Let me practise. There's time, before dinner. Please, Torvald, sit down and play for me. Play, and watch, and put me right.

HELMER. Of course. Whatever you like.

He sits at the piano. NORA *takes a tambourine and a long shawl out of the box. She drapes herself in the shawl, jumps centre front and cries:*

NORA. I'm ready! Play!

HELMER *plays and she dances.* RANK *looks on, standing by the piano.*

HELMER. Slower, slower.

NORA. This way.

HELMER. Not so violently.

NORA. Yes. Yes.

HELMER *stops playing.*

HELMER. It isn't right.

NORA (*laughing, swinging the tambourine*). I *told* you.

RANK. Let me play.

HELMER (*getting up*). Good idea. I'll be able to see better.

RANK *sits and plays.* NORA *dances, ever more wildly.*

HELMER *has taken his place by the stove, and directs her as she dances. She seems not to hear him. Her hair falls over her shoulders, and she pays no attention. She is engrossed in the dance.* MRS LINDE *comes in, and stands at the door, amazed.*

MRS LINDE. Ah!

NORA (*as she dances*). Look, Kristine, look!

HELMER. Nora, darling, anyone'd think your life depended on this dance.

NORA. It does.

HELMER. Rank, stop. This is ridiculous. Stop.

RANK *stops playing, and* NORA *stands suddenly still.* HELMER *goes to her.*

It's incredible. You've forgotten the whole thing.

NORA (*throwing down the tambourine*). I *told* you.

HELMER. You need a lot of practice.

NORA. Yes, Torvald. I must practise, and you must watch. Like you did before. Please, Torvald, please.

HELMER. I said I would.

NORA. Today, tomorrow, concentrate on me. Nothing else. No letters. Don't even open the postbox.

HELMER. You're still afraid of him.

NORA. Yes.

HELMER. He's written a letter. It's here.

NORA. I don't know. I think so. But don't read it. Not now. Nothing nasty must come between us, not now, not now.

RANK (*aside to* HELMER). Better humour her.

HELMER (*taking her in his arms*). Whatever my darling wants.
  But tomorrow night, when you've done your dancing –

NORA. Then you're free.

MAID (*at the door, right*). Madam, dinner's served.

NORA. We'll have champagne, Helene.

MAID. Yes, madam.

  She goes.

HELMER. What do I hear? A celebration?

NORA. A banquet, all night long. Champagne! (*calling.*) And
  macaroons, Helene. Platefuls of macaroons!

  HELMER *takes her hands.*

HELMER. Calm down. Sh, sh. Little singing bird, there there.

NORA. Go in. You too, Doctor. Kristine, help me put up my
  hair.

RANK (*to* HELMER *as they go in*). She's not . . . ah . . . ?

HELMER. No, no, no. My dear fellow! Over-excited, that's
  all.

  They go out, right.

NORA. Well?

MRS LINDE. Gone. Out of town.

NORA. I knew. As soon as I saw you.

MRS LINDE. He'll be back tomorrow afternoon. I wrote him
  a note.

NORA. I wish you hadn't. You can't stop it. A miracle's going to happen, and we're celebrating.

MRS LINDE. What miracle?

NORA. You can't guess. Go in. I won't be long.

MRS LINDE goes into the dining room. NORA stands quite still, as if gathering herself. Then she looks at her watch.

Five o'clock. Seven hours till midnight. Then twenty-four hours till tomorrow midnight. Twenty-four and seven. Thirty-one. Thirty-one hours left, to live.

HELMER comes to the door, right.

HELMER. What's keeping my little singing bird?

NORA. Here she is! Here!

She runs to him with open arms.

Curtain

Act Three

The same. The table and chairs have been moved centre. There is a lighted lamp on the table. The hall door is open, and dance-music can be heard from the upstairs apartment. MRS LINDE is sitting at the table, turning the pages of a book. She is trying to read, but finds it hard to concentrate. She looks at her watch.

MRS LINDE. Still not. It's almost time. Perhaps he won't –

She listens again.

Here he is.

She goes into the hall and carefully opens the main door. Light steps can be heard on the stairs outside. She whispers:

Come in. There's no one here.

KROGSTAD (*in the doorway*). You left me a note. What is it?

MRS LINDE. I must talk to you.

KROGSTAD. Here?

MRS LINDE. Not at my lodgings: I don't have my own entrance. Come in. There's no one here. The servants are asleep, and the Helmers are upstairs at a party.

KROGSTAD (*coming in*). A party? Tonight of all nights?

MRS LINDE. Why shouldn't they?

KROGSTAD. No reason.

MRS LINDE. Nils, we've got to talk.

KROGSTAD. Do we?

MRS LINDE. It's important.

KROGSTAD. Really?

MRS LINDE. You've never understood.

KROGSTAD. What's to understand? It was obvious to anyone. A heartless woman, jilting a man as soon as a better chance turned up.

MRS LINDE. Heartless? D'you really think so? You think it was easy?

KROGSTAD. Wasn't it?

MRS LINDE. You really thought so?

KROGSTAD. If it wasn't, why did you write . . . what you wrote?

MRS LINDE. What else could I do? I had to break with you. It was essential to kill everything you felt for me.

KROGSTAD (*wringing his hands*). Yes. I see. And all that . . . for money.

MRS LINDE. I'd a bedridden mother and two small brothers. We couldn't wait for you, Nils. You'd no prospects then.

KROGSTAD. You'd no right to throw me away for someone else.

MRS LINDE. Who can judge?

KROGSTAD (*slowly*). When I lost you, it was like being shipwrecked. Look: I'm drowning.

MRS LINDE. Help may be near.

KROGSTAD. It was near, until you came and interfered.

MRS LINDE. Until today, I'd no idea it was your job they were giving me.

KROGSTAD. If you say so. But now you know. What will you do now – turn it down?

MRS LINDE. That wouldn't help you.

KROGSTAD. What's help to do with it?

MRS LINDE. Life, hard need . . . I've learned.

KROGSTAD. And I've learned to distrust fancy speeches.

MRS LINDE. Fine words, yes. But deeds?

KROGSTAD. What d'you mean?

MRS LINDE. You said you were drowning.

KROGSTAD. It's true.

MRS LINDE. Well, so am I. No one to weep for, to care for.

KROGSTAD. You chose it.

MRS LINDE. I had to – then.

KROGSTAD. What d'you mean?

MRS LINDE. Nils, two drowning people – can't we help each other?

KROGSTAD. You –

MRS LINDE. Two together, support each other.

KROGSTAD. Kristine.

MRS LINDE. Why else d'you think I came?

KROGSTAD. You thought of me?

MRS LINDE. All my life, as long as I can remember, I've worked. It's been my greatest pleasure, my only pleasure. Now I'm alone . . . empty, thrown away. Where's the satisfaction in working for oneself? Nils, give me someone, something to work for.

KROGSTAD. Hysteria. Female hysteria. Extravagant self-sacrifice, that's what this is.

MRS LINDE. From *me*?

KROGSTAD. You know . . . all about me? My past?

MRS LINDE. Yes.

KROGSTAD. And what I count for here?

MRS LINDE. You said just now, hinted, that if I'd been with you things would have been different.

KROGSTAD. Quite different.

MRS LINDE. And now?

KROGSTAD. Kristine, you mean this. I can see it. You really would –

MRS LINDE. I need someone to mother; your children need a mother; you and I need each other. I trust you, Nils, the man you really are.

KROGSTAD (*taking her hands*). Thankyou. Kristine, thankyou.

Now I can . . . climb again. No. I forgot . . .

MRS LINDE. Sh! The tarantella. Go, now.

KROGSTAD. What?

MRS LINDE. As soon as it's done, they'll be coming.

KROGSTAD. I'll go. But there's nothing we can do. You don't know what . . . steps I've taken with the Helmers.

MRS LINDE. Nils, I do.

KROGSTAD. And still you – ?

MRS LINDE. Despair – I know what it makes people do.

KROGSTAD. If I could only cancel it.

MRS LINDE. You can. Your letter's still there, in the box at the door.

KROGSTAD (*giving her a long look*). It's her you want to save. Your friend. That's what this is.

MRS LINDE. Nils, someone who's sold herself once for someone else, doesn't do it twice.

KROGSTAD. I'll ask for my letter back.

MRS LINDE. No.

KROGSTAD. Yes. I'll wait for Helmer. I'll tell him I want my letter . . . it's just about my dismissal . . . he's not to read it . . .

MRS LINDE. No, Nils. You mustn't. Don't ask for it back.

KROGSTAD. That's why you wrote, why you asked me here.

MRS LINDE. It was, yesterday. I was in a panic. But since then, you won't believe the sights I've seen in this house. Helmer must know the truth. The secret must come out. No more lies, tricks, they must understand each other.

KROGSTAD. Whatever you say. But there's one thing I can do, and I'll do it now.

MRS LINDE (*listening*). Hurry. Go. They've finished. We're not safe a moment longer.

KROGSTAD. I'll wait downstairs.

MRS LINDE. Yes: they may see me to the door.

KROGSTAD. This is the luckiest day of my life!

He goes out through the hall, leaving the hall door open. MRS LINDE *tidies the room, and puts her coat ready to put on.*

MRS LINDE. At last. Someone to work for, live for. A home. There. It's all I want. If only they'd *come.*

She listens.

They're here. Coat on.

HELMER *and* NORA *can be heard off. Key in the door, then* HELMER *all but pulls* NORA *into the hall. She is wearing the Itlian dress and a large black shawl; he is in evening dress, with a black, swirling cloak.* NORA *stands in the doorway, resisting.*

NORA. No. No. I want to go back up. It's too soon, too soon.

HELMER. Nora, darling –

NORA. Please, Torvald. Please. Another hour. For little Nora. Please.

HELMER. No, darling. Not another minute. We agreed. Go
    in. You'll catch cold out here.

She still resists, but he brings her into the room.

MRS LINDE. Good evening.

NORA. Kristine!

HELMER. Mrs Linde, good evening. Isn't it rather late – ?

MRS LINDE. I'm sorry. I was dying to see Nora in her dress.

NORA. You've been sitting, waiting?

MRS LINDE. I just missed you, you'd gone upstairs. I
    couldn't go home again without seeing you.

HELMER (*taking off* NORA's *shawl*). Well, here she is. Isn't
    she pretty? Isn't she delightful?

MRS LINDE. She's –

HELMER. They all thought so, upstairs. But what an
    obstinate little thing it is. What are we to do with her?
    D'you know, I almost had to steal her away by force.

NORA. Torvald, it would have been all right. Just half an
    hour.

HELMER. You see, Mrs Linde? She danced her tarantella. A
    triumph. As well it should have been. A little . . . energetic,
    a little more . . . enthusiastic than artistic . . . but still a
    triumph. Was I going to let her stay after that? Spoil the
    effect? Of course I wasn't. I took my little Capri fishergirl –
    my delicious, capricious little fishergirl – on my arm . . .
    swift tour round the room, curtsey here, curtsey there –
    and the vision of loveliness was gone, as they say in fairy

tales. Always make a good exit, Mrs Linde – that's what I keep telling her. Fff, it's hot in here.

He throws his cloak over a chair, and opens the study door.

Dark? It's dark. Excuse me.

He goes into the study and lights a couple of candles. Meanwhile, NORA *whispers to* MRS LINDE, *quickly and breathlessly:*

NORA. Well?

MRS LINDE (*in a low voice*). I've talked to him.

NORA. And – ?

MRS LINDE. Nora, you must tell Torvald. Everything.

NORA (*tonelessly*). I knew it.

MRS LINDE. You've nothing to fear from Krogstad. But you must tell Torvald.

NORA. I won't do it.

MRS LINDE. Then the letter will.

NORA. Thanks, Kristine. Now the miracle – Sh!

HELMER (*coming back in*). Well, Mrs Linde? Have you gazed your fill?

MRS LINDE. I'll say goodnight.

HELMER. Is this yours, this knitting?

MRS LINDE (*taking it*). I'd forgotten all about it.

HELMER. You knit as well?

MRS LINDE. Yes.

HELMER. Have you ever tried embroidery?

MRS LINDE. Why?

HELMER. Far more becoming. Look, when you embroider, you hold the frame like this, in the left hand, the needle like this, in the right hand . . . a graceful, easy movement . . .

MRS LINDE. Yes.

HELMER. Whereas knitting . . . no gracefulness . . . elbows in, needles pumping up and down . . . chopsticks . . . That was wonderful champagne.

MRS LINDE. Good night, Nora. And no more obstinate.

HELMER. Well said!

MRS LINDE. Good night, sir.

HELMER (*going to the door with her*). Good night, good night. You'll find your way home? I could easily . . . no, it's just round the corner. Good night, good night.

She goes, and he shuts the door and comes back into the room.

What a boring woman!

NORA. Torvald, you must be tired.

HELMER. Not at all.

NORA. Sleepy?

HELMER. Wide awake, full of beans. What about you? You look exhausted.

NORA. I must go to bed.

HELMER. You see! I was right, to make you come away.

NORA. You're always right.

HELMER (*kissing her forehead*). That's it. Little singing bird, making lots of sense. Did you notice Rank this evening? How happy he was?

NORA. I hardly spoke to him.

HELMER. Neither did I. But I've seldom seen him so jolly.

He looks at her for a moment, then goes closer.

H'm. It's so nice to be back home again, just the two of us. Just you, and me.

NORA. Torvald.

HELMER. My darling. No one else's. My sweetheart, my treasure.

NORA *goes to the other side of the table.*

NORA. Don't look at me like that.

HELMER (*following her*). Aha! Little Miss Tarantella still? More delicious than ever. Listen! The guests are leaving. (*in a low voice.*) Nora, soon it'll be so still, so still . . .

NORA. I hope so.

HELMER. Darling, you know when I'm out with you, at a party, when I hardly talk to you, just glance at you now and then – d'you know why I do that? I'm pretending we're secret lovers, that we're promised to one another, and it's our secret, no one knows but us.

NORA. I know you were thinking of me.

HELMER. When it's time to come away, and I'm arranging

the shawl on your pretty shoulders, your lovely neck, I imagine you're my new young bride, we've just come from the wedding, I'm bringing you home for the very first time . . . we're alone for the very first time . . . alone, my shy little, sweet little darling. All evening I've longed for nothing else but you. When I saw you twirling, swirling in the tarantella, my blood pounded, I couldn't bear it, I hurried you, hurried you down here –

NORA. Torvald! Let me go! I won't!

HELMER. Darling, you're joking, it's a game. Won't? Won't? I'm your husband.

Knock at the outer door.

NORA (*startled*). Listen!

HELMER (*at the hall door*). Who is it?

RANK (*off*). Me. Can I come in a moment?

HELMER (*low, crossly*). What does he want? (*aloud.*) Just a minute.

He goes and opens the door.

Nice of you to drop by.

RANK. I thought I heard you. Just wanted to make sure.

He glances all round.

Yes, yes. These dear, familiar rooms. Such a happy, cosy little home.

HELMER. I see you enjoyed the party too.

RANK. Of course. Why shouldn't I? Why shouldn't we enjoy

every blessed thing? As much as we can, as long as we can. Good wine –

HELMER. Especially champagne.

RANK. I was amazed how much I managed to put away.

NORA. Torvald drank plenty too.

RANK. Really?

NORA. It goes straight to his head, always.

RANK. No harm in a . . . jolly evening after a well-spent day.

HELMER. Well-spent? I can't quite claim that.

RANK (*slapping his back*). But I can, I can.

NORA. Scientific work, Doctor Rank? Investigation?

RANK. Exactly.

HELMER. Such big words for such a little girl! Scientific . . . investigation . . .

NORA. May I congratulate you on the result?

RANK. Indeed you may.

NORA. A good one?

RANK. For the doctor, and the patient, the very best.

NORA (*eagerly, anxiously*). Final?

RANK. Final. So didn't I deserve a jolly evening, after that?

NORA. Oh doctor, of course you did.

HELMER. Hear, hear. So long as you don't regret it in the morning.

RANK. No one must ever regret anything, ever.

NORA. You really enjoy fancy-dress parties?

RANK. If there are plenty of pretty costumes.

NORA. So what will we go as next time, you and I?

HELMER. Little featherbrain, thinking of next time already.

RANK. You and I? I know: you can be a good-luck pixie.

HELMER. What on Earth will she wear for that?

RANK. Just her ordinary clothes.

HELMER. Bravo! How gallant! And what will you go as?

RANK. I know, exactly.

HELMER. What?

RANK. At the next fancy-dress party, I shall be – invisible.

HELMER. Brilliant!

RANK. There's a big black hat – haven't you heard of it?
    You put it on . . . invisible.

HELMER (*checking a smile*). Absolutely right.

RANK. But I'm forgetting what I came for. Helmer, give me
    a cigar, one of the dark Havanas.

HELMER. Delighted.

He offers him the case. RANK *takes a cigar and cuts the end.*

NORA (*striking a match*). Let me light it for you.

RANK. Thankyou.

He holds out the cigar, and she lights it.

And now, goodbye.

HELMER. Goodbye, dear old friend, goodbye.

NORA. Sleep well, Doctor.

RANK. Thankyou.

NORA. Say the same to me.

RANK. If you like. Sleep well. And thanks for the light.

He nods to them both, and goes out.

HELMER (*glumly*). Too much to drink.

NORA (*absently*). Perhaps.

HELMER *takes keys out of his pocket and goes into the hall.*

Torvald! What are you doing?

HELMER. The letter box is full. If I don't clear it, they'll never get the papers in tomorrow.

NORA. You're not going to work tonight.

HELMER. You know I'm not. Hello. Someone's been at the lock.

NORA. The lock?

HELMER. Yes. But who? Not the servants . . . A broken hairpin. Yours, Nora.

NORA (*quickly*). One of the children must have –

HELMER. Make sure they never do it again. Hm, hm . . . there. Done it.

He takes the letters out and shouts to the kitchen.

Helene! Helene! Put out the front door lamp.

He comes in and shuts the hall door. He has the letters in his hand.

Just look at them all.

He turns them over.

What's this?

NORA (*at the window*). No, Torvald!

HELMER. Two visiting cards – from Rank.

NORA. Rank?

HELMER (*looking at the cards*). Lars Johan Rank, Bachelor of Medicine. They were on top. He must have posted them when he went out just now.

NORA. Is there anything on them?

HELMER. A cross of some kind, over the name. Look. What an odd idea. You'd think he was announcing his own death.

NORA. He was.

HELMER. You know about this? He told you?

NORA. He said, when the card came, it was to say goodbye. He'll lock himself in, to die.

HELMER. My friend. My poor friend. I knew we wouldn't have him long. But so soon, and shutting himself away like a wounded animal.

NORA. If it has to happen, it's better without a word. Don't you think so?

HELMER (*pacing*). He was like family. I can't imagine him . . . gone. Unhappy, lonely – he was like the sky, and our happiness was the Sun. Well, perhaps it's best. For him, anyway. (*standing still.*) And perhaps for us too, Nora. We've no one else now, just each other.

He puts his arms round her.

Darling wife, I can never hold you tight enough. D'you know, I've often wished you were in some deadly danger, so that I could give my heart's blood, my life, for you.

NORA (*firmly, disengaging herself*). You must open those letters, Torvald.

HELMER. Not tonight. I want to be with you, darling. With my wife.

NORA. But Rank, think of Rank –

HELMER. Yes. It's come between us – ugliness, death, a reminder of death. We must try to shake it off. Till then – separate rooms.

NORA *throws her arms round him.*

NORA. Darling, sleep well, sleep well.

HELMER (*kissing her forehead*). Sleep well, little songbird. Sleep well, Nora. I'll read those letters now.

He takes the letters into the study and shuts the door. NORA, *wild-eyed, fumbles round, takes his cloak and throws it round herself. She speaks in a hoarse, broken whisper.*

NORA. Never again. Never see him again. Never.

She puts her shawl over her head.

The children . . . never again. Never. Water . . . deep . . . black . . . Soon, soon, if only . . . He's opened it. He's reading it. Nothing, now. Torvald, little ones, goodbye –

She is about to hurry out through the hall, when HELMER *opens the study door and stands there. He holds an open letter.*

HELMER. Nora.

NORA (*scream*). Ah!

HELMER. You know what this letter says?

NORA. I know. Let me go. Let me out.

HELMER. Where are you going?

He holds her back. She struggles.

NORA. You won't save me, Torvald.

HELMER (*stumbling*). It's true? What he writes, it's true? Unbearable. It's not, it can't be –

NORA. It's true. You were more than all the world to me.

HELMER. Never . . . mind . . . that.

NORA (*going to him*). Torvald!

HELMER. How could you?

NORA. Let me go. Don't help me. Don't take it over. Please.

HELMER. Stop playing games.

He locks the hall door.

You're staying. You have to come to terms. D'you understand what you've done? Do you understand?

NORA (*looking straight at him; frost forming in her voice*). Now, I understand.

HELMER (*pacing*). To wake up to this! Eight years . . . my joy, my life, my wife . . . Lies, deceit . . . a criminal. No way out. No end.

He stops and looks at her. She returns his gaze, without a word.

I should have expected it. I should have known. Like father – sh! – like daughter. No religion, no ethics, no sense of duty. I shut my eyes to what he was like – for your sake, for you – and this is what I get. This is how you repay me.

NORA. This is how I repay you.

HELMER. You've killed my happiness. You've destroyed my future. I'm trapped, in his claws. No mercy. He'll do whatever he likes to me, demand, insist, I can't refuse. No way out. A silly, empty-headed woman – and now I'm dead.

NORA. When I'm out of your way, you'll be free of it.

HELMER. Don't . . . talk. Your father was just the same. Talk! Even if you're out of the way, as you put it, what good is that to me? He'll tell his tale. They'll think I knew what you were doing, that I was part of it. Behind it, even – that the whole thing was my idea. And this from you, the wife I supported and cherished throughout our marriage. Now d'you understand what you've done to me?

NORA (*icy*). Entirely.

HELMER. It's beyond belief. I can't believe it. But it's happened; we have to cope with it. Take off that shawl. Take it off! I must try and calm him. It *must* be hushed up. Whatever it costs. As for you and me, we must go on as if nothing had changed between us. In public. You'll stay on

here, obviously. But I won't have you near the children.
I can never trust you again. Fancy having to say that to
you – the woman I loved, I still . . . no. It's gone.
Happiness is gone. Rags, crumbs, pretence . . .

Doorbell, off. He jumps.

At this hour? It can't be, not *him*. Nora, hide yourself. Say
you're ill.

She stands motionless. He unlocks the hall door. The MAID *is in the
hall, in her nightclothes.*

MAID. A letter. For madam.

HELMER. Give it me.

He takes the letter and shuts the door.

Yes. It's from him. Leave it. I'll read it.

NORA. You read it.

HELMER (*by the lamp*). I . . . can't. It could be the end of us,
both of us. No, I must.

He tears open the letter, reads a few lines, then shouts with joy:

Nora!

NORA *looks at him enquiringly.*

Nora . . . no, just let me check. Yes, yes. I'm saved. Nora,
I'm saved.

NORA. And me?

HELMER. You as well. Naturally. Both of us are saved. He's
sent your contract back. Writes that he's sorry . . . his life
has changed . . . what does it matter what he writes? We're

saved. No one can touch you. Nora, Nora – wait. First these must be got rid of. H'm . . .

He glances at the contract.

No, I won't look at it. Forget it, a nightmare.

He tears the document and the letters in pieces, stuffs them in the stove and watches while they burn.

There you are: finished. He said that ever since Christmas Eve you've – Nora, these last three days have been dreadful for you.

NORA. I've fought hard these last three days.

HELMER. Racking yourself, no way out – no, don't let's think about it. It was dreadful; it's over; let's shout for joy. Nora, don't you understand? It's over. What's the matter? Such an icy face. Oh darling, Nora, I know what it is. You can't believe I've forgiven you. I have, I promise. Forgiven you everything. I know that everything you did, you did because you loved me.

NORA. Yes.

HELMER. You loved me as all wives should love their husbands. You were new to it, that's all: you didn't understand what you were doing. But don't think I love you any less, just because you don't know how to manage things. I'll guide you, darling, I'll protect you. Lean on me. I'd hardly be a man, if feminine weakness, your weakness, didn't make me love you even more. Those hard words, when I thought everything was lost – forget them. I've forgiven you, Nora, I swear I've forgiven you.

NORA. You're very kind.

She goes out, right.

HELMER. Wait. (*looking in.*) What are you doing?

NORA (*off*). Changing. No more fancy dress.

HELMER (*at the open door*). Yes. Good. Be calm, be calm, my
frightened little bird. Nothing will hurt you; I'll spread my
wings, I'll shelter you. (*pacing by the door.*) It's warm and
cosy, our nest, our home. Nothing will hurt you. Poor
frightened dove, I'll save you from the hawk, I'll keep you
safe. Still, little fluttering heart, be still. It'll be all right.
Darling, you'll see. Tomorrow . . . it'll all be like it was
before. You'll soon understand, I won't need to remind you
I've forgiven you. I'll never abandon you, never blame you
– how can you think so? A husband's love, darling – a true
husband's heart, how can you understand it? How sweet,
how satisfying, to feel that he's forgiven his wife, from the
depths of his being, forgiven her? Made her twice his own:
given her life, identity, his wife, his child. That's what you
are to me now, poor, helpless little darling. Don't ever be
frightened, Nora. Tell me the truth, and your will, your
conscience – leave both to me. But what – ? Not going to
bed? You've changed.

NORA (*in her ordinary clothes*). I've changed.

HELMER. But why now? It's late.

NORA. I won't sleep tonight.

HELMER. Nora, darling –

NORA (*looking at her watch*). It's not very late. Sit here,
Torvald. We have to come to terms.

She sits at one side of the table.

HELMER. Nora? So cold –

NORA. Sit down. There's a lot to say.

HELMER *sits facing her across the table.*

HELMER. Nora? I don't understand.

NORA. Exactly. You don't understand me. And I've never understood you – until just now. Don't say anything. Listen. It's time to come to terms.

HELMER. What d'you mean?

NORA (*after a short pause*). It's strange. Isn't it?

HELMER. What is?

NORA. We've been married eight years. And this is the first time we've sat down together, you and me, husband and wife, to talk seriously.

HELMER. Seriously.

NORA. In eight years – no, since the first day we met – we've never talked seriously about a single thing.

HELMER. You didn't expect me to tell you my worries all the time – things you couldn't help me with?

NORA. I don't mean, business. I mean, we've never sat down and settled anything.

HELMER. Darling, that wasn't your way.

NORA. That's it exactly. You've never understood me. You've done me great wrong, Torvald – you, and Daddy before you.

HELMER. The two men who loved you most in all the world?

NORA (*shaking her head*). You never loved me. Either of you. It pleased you, that's all – the idea of loving me.

HELMER. What are you telling me?

NORA. The truth, Torvald. When I lived with Daddy, he told me his views on everything, so I shared his views. If I disagreed I didn't say so: he'd have hated it. He called me his little dolly-baby, and played with me as I played with my dollies. Then I came here, to you –

HELMER. Is that how you describe our marriage?

NORA (*calmly*). I was transferred from Daddy's care to yours. You organised everything to suit yourself: your taste. So I shared your taste, or pretended to, I'm not sure which. Perhaps both: sometimes one, sometimes the other. I realise it now: I lived here hand to mouth, like a beggar. I've existed to perform for you, Torvald. That's what you wanted. You've done me great harm, you and Daddy: you've blocked my life.

HELMER. You're unreasonable, Nora, ungrateful. Haven't you been happy here?

NORA. No, never. I thought I was, but I wasn't.

HELMER. Not . . . happy . . . ?

NORA. Cheerful. You've always been kind to me. But it's as if we live in a Wendy house. I'm your dolly-wife, just as I used to be Daddy's dolly-baby. And my dolls were the children. When you played with me, I had a lovely time – and so did they when I played with them. That's our marriage, Torvald. That's what it's been like.

HELMER. Maybe you're right. Hysterical, overwrought, but a little bit right. And now things are going to change. Playtime ends; lessons begin.

NORA. Mine? Or the children's?

HELMER. Darling, yours *and* theirs.

NORA. Torvald, how could *you* ever teach me to be a proper wife? Your wife?

HELMER. You're joking.

NORA. And how could I ever teach the children?

HELMER. Nora!

NORA. You said so yourself just now. You'd never trust me again.

HELMER. I'd lost my temper. Surely, you didn't think I meant it?

NORA. It was the truth. I can't bring them up. I've someone else to bring up first – myself. You can't help. I must do it myself. That's why I'm leaving you.

HELMER (*jumping up*). What?

NORA. If I'm to come to terms with myself, understand myself, I have to be alone. I can't stay here.

HELMER. Nora, Nora.

NORA. I'll go right away. I'll sleep at Kristine's tonight.

HELMER. You're mad. I forbid this.

NORA. No more forbidding. I'll take what belongs to me. I need nothing of yours, either now or later.

HELMER. You're out of your mind.

NORA. Tomorrow I'll go home – I mean, where I was born. I'll find something there.

HELMER. You're blind. You don't know how –

NORA. I'll find out how.

HELMER. Deserting your home, your husband, your children. What will people say?

NORA. I must. Let them say what they like.

HELMER. It's unbelievable. You abandon your most sacred obligations –

NORA. You know what they are, then, my sacred obligations?

HELMER. You need me to tell you? To your husband, your children.

NORA. I've other obligations, just as sacred.

HELMER. Of course you haven't. What obligations?

NORA. To myself.

HELMER. You're a wife, a mother. They come first.

NORA. I don't think so, now. Not any more. I think that first I'm a human being, the same as you. Or at least that I'll try to be one. I know that most people would agree with you, Torvald, that that's what they teach in books. But I've had enough of what most people say, what they write in books. It's not enough. I must think things out for myself, I must decide.

HELMER. You should think about your place, here in your own home. Have you nothing to guide you? No . . . belief?

NORA. I don't know what that is.

HELMER. What?

NORA. All I know is what Pastor Hansen taught at confirmation class. Belief is this, and this, he said. I'll think about it, when I've time, when I've gone away. Work out if Pastor Hansen's belief was right – for me.

HELMER. You're a girl, a child! If belief doesn't affect you, what about conscience? Morality? Or have you none of that?

NORA. I can't answer. I don't know. I'm baffled. All I know is, you and I have different ideas about it all. And the law – I've discovered that's not what I always thought it was, and I can't believe it's right. A woman mustn't spare her dying father, or save her husband's life. I can't believe it.

HELMER. You're talking like a child. You don't understand the society you live in.

NORA. You're right: I don't. But I'm going to find out – which of us is right, society or me.

HELMER. Nora, you're ill. You're delirious. I think you're raving.

NORA. I've never felt better. My mind's never been clearer.

HELMER. Clearer? Leaving your husband, your children – ?

NORA. That's what I'm doing.

HELMER. There's only one explanation.

NORA. What?

HELMER. You've stopped loving me.

NORA. That's it exactly.

HELMER. How can you say that?

NORA. It hurts, Torvald. You've always been wonderful to me. But I can't help it. I've just stopped loving you.

HELMER (*controlling himself*). Something else you're clear about?

NORA. Completely clear. It's why I'm going.

HELMER. And what did I do? To lose your love? Can you tell me that?

NORA. It was tonight. The miracle didn't happen. I saw you weren't the man I'd imagined.

HELMER. You're not making sense.

NORA. For eight years I've waited patiently. Miracles don't happen every day, God knows. Then I was engulfed in catastrophe, and I was certain: it'll happen now, the miracle. When Krogstad sent his letter, I was certain you'd never give in to him. You'd tell him to publish and be damned. And then –

HELMER. When I'd exposed my own wife to disgrace and shame – ?

NORA. Then, I was certain, you'd take the whole thing on your own shoulders, and say, 'I did it. I was the guilty one.'

HELMER. Nora – !

NORA. You think I'd have denied it? Of course I would. But what would my word have been worth, compared with yours? That was the miracle I hoped for – and it was to prevent it that I was going to kill myself.

HELMER. Darling, I'd work night and day for you. I'd endure starvation, agony. But no man sacrifices his *honour* for the one he loves.

NORA. Hundreds of thousands of women do just that.

HELMER. You're talking – thinking – like a child.

NORA. Perhaps. But you're not talking or thinking like t' husband I long for. As soon as you stopped panicking panicking for me, but for what might happen to you when it was over, you behaved as if nothing at all ha happened. So far as you were concerned, I went bac what I'd always been: your pet bird, your doll, whic now have to treat with extra care because I was fra breakable. (*getting up.*) That's when I realised, Torv eight years I've lived with a stranger. Borne him t' children. I can't bear it. I'd like to tear myself to [

HELMER (*heavily*). It's clear. It's clear. There's a gu up between us. But surely we can bridge it, fill it

NORA. The woman I am now is no wife for you.

HELMER. I'll change. I can change –

NORA. If your doll's taken away, perhaps.

HELMER. Nora. Don't leave me. I don't under

NORA. That's why I must.

She goes into the room right, and comes back with her cloak and hat and a small suitcase, which she puts on the chair by the table.

HELMER. Not tonight. Tomorrow.

NORA (*putting on her cloak*). I can't spend the night in a strange man's house.

HELMER. Brother and sister? Can't we live like that?

NORA (*putting on her hat*). It wouldn't last. You know that.

She puts on the shawl.

Goodbye, Torvald. I don't want to see the children. They're in better hands than mine. The woman I am now can do nothing for them.

HELMER. One day, Nora, one day – ?

NORA. How can I answer? I don't know what I'll be.

HELMER. Whatever you'll be, whatever you are, you're still my wife.

NORA. Torvald, listen to me. When a wife deserts her husband, as I'm deserting you, the law frees him of all obligations towards her. And in any case, I set you free. You're not bound in any way. You're free. We're both free. On both sides: freedom. Take back your ring. Give me mine.

HELMER. That too?

NORA. That too.

HELMER. There.

NORA. Thankyou. It's over. I'll put the keys here. The servants know where everything is – better than I do. Tomorrow, as soon as I've left the town, Kristine will come and pack my things – my own things, the things I brought from home. I'll have them sent on.

HELMER. Over. Over. Nora, won't you ever think of me?

NORA. Often. You, the children, this house –

HELMER. Can I write to you?

NORA. No. It's forbidden.

HELMER. I could send you –

NORA. Nothing.

HELMER. If you needed help –

NORA. I'll take nothing from a stranger.

HELMER. Will I never be more to you?

NORA (*taking the case*). If the miracle happened –

HELMER. Tell me the miracle.

NORA. If we changed, both of us, if we – No, Torvald. I've stopped believing in miracles.

HELMER. I believe. Tell me. If we changed, if we –

NORA. If we discovered some true relationship. Goodbye.

She goes out through the hall. HELMER *slumps into a chair by the door and covers his face.*

HELMER. Nora! Nora!

He gets up, looks round.

Empty. She's gone.

A hope flashes across his face.

A miracle – ?

A door slams, off.

Final Curtain

NOTES

NOTES

NOTES

NOTES